N ‖‖‖‖‖‖‖‖‖‖‖‖ P
MW01291339

How To Be A Strong Man In A Weak World

Charles Sledge

Table Of Contents

Introduction

We live in an age when masculinity is under attack. Never have males been more effeminate, weak, and perhaps worst of all proud of it. The modern male has lost his warrior spirit, that fire that animated him to achieve great deeds in ages past.

Now we live in a time when everything is neutered and sanitized until there is nothing left. Boys are taught that their masculinity is evil and is something that they should be ashamed of. Because of this we have a generation of weak effeminate cucks.

We have male feminists, white knights, and a whole host of other evils that plague our society. The truth of the matter is that most of these males never had any guidance. They never had a strong father figure who told them to "man up" or more importantly how to go about doing so.

The world is crying out for masculinity and yet little is to be found. To be a masculine man in this age is to be a great beacon of light in a dark stormy sea. A beacon that can show others the way.

Those that cannot be saved will be declared war on however there can be no victory until masculinity is restored throughout the lands.

It is masculinity that brings order out of chaos. And the good kind of order not the slave order that society would push on males. Confining them to cubicles, having to keep their balls in their wives purse, as well as keeping their thoughts within certain boundaries. That is not order but rather slavery under the guise of order.

However even if you were never given guidance on being a man you can still become one. Even if your father abandoned you and your society has left you for dead if you do not choose slavery you can still make it. You can still be a free masculine man in a world of weak effeminate slaves and their masters.

You can be the barbarian, the warrior, and the king that you know you were meant to be. There is a spark deep inside that knows this. Depending on who you are and how conditioned you have been this spark may be down deep. But nevertheless it is there and this spark can turn into a blazing fire if given the right fuel.

Well this book is the right fuel. The fuel that will turn that heated coal into a raging inferno of greatness. It's time to reclaim your masculinity, it's time to reclaim your freedom. Life is too short and too precious to spend any part of it a slave.

Heed the call. The ancient primal call that comes from your creator and that your very blood cries out for. You were meant to live with a fire in your heart. To be a man fully and completely. That is you task in life. Because trust me when you become a man fully and completely everything else will fall into place.

Now join me on the most important journey you will ever undertake. A journey to reclaim your masculinity.

Embracing The "I Am Dominant" Frame

What does it mean to be dominant? While there are many facets to dominance. The different types of dominance have an underlying similarity. Specifically that they have to do with your reality being stronger than the others. This can be cultivated even to the point where you shape the very world around you. No I'm not talking about psychic powers or any such nonsense. I'm talking using your mind to create the life of your dreams.

Being dominant is about having a stronger frame or version of reality than others. So for a simplified example let's say that you think you're great. You meet a girl who looks at you and says your trash. A guy with no dominance and a weak frame would apologize for "being trash" or react emotionally while agreeing with her subconsciously. A guy with a strong frame and sense of dominance would either ignore her completely or laugh at her faulty attempts to faze him.

This is the mindset that you should have. In any situation that you are dominant. This doesn't mean domineering where you wade your way into everyone's space and make demands of them. Rather than your frame and the way you see things remain the dominant focal point of your mind.

In Social Settings

Well use a party as an example. Let's say you're at a party in high school. You just moved in from out of town and were invited by some girl who went into some room with a guy and you haven't seen her in a while nor expect to. It's just you, you don't know anything else. Now let's say you see a cute girl surrounded in a corner surrounded by a bunch of guys.

A guy with a dominant mindset would go over and talk to her. As his desire to do so would be more important to him than being judged by others. A guy with a submissive mindset would try to make friends with everyone first then be "allowed" to talk to the girl. He wouldn't go straight after what he wants, he would go about in a roundabout way. Which is feminine and submissive behavior.

The point is you should always consider your frame of reference the most important one. You're at a party, you think you're great, awesome. Talk to whoever you want, flirty with whoever you want, operate uninhibitedly as a freeman. Don't let others shame you into a corner or accept their version of reality if it differs from yours. Do so and people will eventually come around to your version of reality. They may resist it at first but the weak have docile minds and will always give in to someone who knows in which direction they are headed. A man with a "I am dominant" mindset.

You're The King

You are the king of your own world. You are the most important person in your own world. You should love yourself and invest in yourself. Care more about what you think of yourself than what others think of you, no matter who those others may be. Let your frame and version of reality be the strongest. Don't give in to what others think. Instead choose your own path and follow it to fruition.

What you think matters most. Others will try to shame you and control you. Don't let them. Nothing and I mean nothing is worth your freedom. You are the captain of your own ship. You control in which direction your life is heading. It is your choice to be a confident dominant man who gets the most out of life or to be another castrated slave, a sheep, shackled to the limited beliefs of society and others.

Break free and reclaim your freedom. Live for yourself that is how it is supposed to be. Treat the world as your own personal domain, for it is. Well that's not entirely accurate as it's not just the world that is your domain but the universe itself. We were created to be creators. To extend our will on the world and reality around us and shape it to how we see fit.

Summary

Assert yourself into the reality of others with your own version always being the strongest. Pierce and dominate the reality of others with your own. Always maintain the frame and have the stronger version of reality. You're the king, never forget this. When others see strength they instinctually test it, especially women. But once they see you won't change for them then they submit to it. Women will generally get turned on and males will either get all pissy you don't give a shit what they think, while men will respect you. Always embrace the "I am dominant" mindset in every situation regardless if it's with work, women, or wherever else. You are dominant.

The Only Way To Get Respect

Despite what your yuppie teachers told you talking will never get you respect. There is only one thing that will get you respect and that is fear and fear is cultivated through force.

The Truth About Society

Despite what everyone will say society is based on force. Nothing more and nothing less. The only reason anyone follows a law is because there is a police force there to enforce the consequences should they break it. The only reason people cooperate with the police force is because they have guns they can use to enforce their will. The only reason certain countries don't invade others is because larger forces may attack them for it.

Force is ultimately what matters. He who has the force has the power and therefore the respect. It has nothing to do with morality or who has the right ideology. Respect derives from being able to use force properly which is where fear comes from. From being dangerous and as a man as I said in The Primer

"A man who ain't dangerous, ain't much of a man"

This will ruffle the feathers of many but it's the truth. If you're not dangerous you can't fully be a man. It's funny people will say an "alpha male" or whatever is someone who is ripped and well-dressed despite neither one of those facets having much to do with masculinity. The basis for society and respect is force.

Fear

You might have this idea that I'm telling you to become some domineering asshole who tries to start a fight with everyone he meets. This is far from the truth. First off someone who looks for fights often finds them and if it was a real fight it isn't something he'll be looking for anytime soon. No I'm telling you that to be a man you must be able to defend yourself and that which you care about whether it is your spouse and country (or not) or your children. They should have respect for you because they know that you are capable of applying a dangerous amount of force. They know that their father, brother, friend, or whatever category you fall into is not someone to be messed with and has the capacity to be dangerous.

Learn to fight and to shoot. There are no exceptions to this. Your gated neighborhoods aren't keeping anyone out for long. Change is coming to America and the rest of the world. You can pretend like violence isn't going to be a part of your life but it will be. If you have sons it is imperative that you teach them to fight. If not they will be weeded out and picked on. The weak of the pack are the ones that are picked off. Don't let it be your offspring. If you are a father and don't teach your sons how to apply force against those who would stand against them or use it against them you have failed them as a father and set them up for a life of pain.

Practical Steps

If you don't have a gun then get one. That's step one. Then learn the proper use of that gun. Learn how to point shoot. Target shooting isn't going to do you much good. Then pick up a martial art of some sort it doesn't matter which as long as you use it with ferocity and intensity. Personally I'm partial to boxing with some Judo or Wrestling mixed in but do what works for you. Make sure that whatever you do you throw in striking and ground work don't neglect either as both are important. And most importantly cultivate the attitude needed to inflict violence on another. Embrace you masculine animalistic instinct and harness it. Violence is part of our world and force is needed, understand this.

Fighting Is A Necessary Skill

Violence. It makes up a fundamental part of our world. Though many have been able to shelter themselves from it, that time is coming to an end. The world is changing. People are being thrown together that have nothing and common and nothing but distrust and hatred for each other. The elites love this as it causes disorder, hatred, and tension. Allowing them to be the heroes that all can supposedly rally to. However in the meantime it will result in more pain, suffering, and death. Which will eventually lead to tyranny.

Not a pretty picture but an accurate one. For many years the vast majority of those living in Western societies have been able to get away with being soft. They were sheltered from violence by strong men who they often hated and lambasted. Now we live in a world where the strong men can only do so much and often won't if it isn't politically correct. Soon you will be on your own. Especially if you are a law abiding citizen who isn't rich or isn't part of a protected class and even then you may not be safe.

I don't say this to project doom and gloom nor to scare you. Though if you have taken no measures to prepare you should feel some source of discomfort. That discomfort you feel now may very well be the thing that saves your life one day. Because it spurned you on to action, it spurned you on to take matters into your own hands. To take responsibility for your safety, because no one else is going to.

Be Dangerous

In The Primer I said "A man who isn't dangerous isn't much of a man" and I stand by that. We have been weakened and are ripe for the plundering which is happening all around us. Look at crime statistics, there is a war going on with real causalities. You could be next if you allow yourself to be a target. It doesn't matter if you live in a gated neighborhood or out in the country you will only be isolated for so long before you will have to deal with the changing realities of the world.

You must become dangerous if you and your kin are going to survive the next fifty years. You best know how to fight. This isn't a suggestion, it's a requirement if you want to live in peace. Remember the only way to prevent war. To be so strong that declaring war on you wouldn't be worth it. That's the only way to keep peace, to be able to beat the living dog shit out of the other guy. Not words, not bribing, and sure as fuck not kindness. But violence. Violence is golden.

Train For Combat

Training is good. While when most think of training they think of weight training which there is nothing wrong with and which I do and recommend wholeheartedly. However there are some stipulations there. You shouldn't train alone for being big or for looks but you should train for something that will be beneficial for you. Train for strength, train for doing damage to others, but don't train simply for vanity like a woman. There should be a point to your training, to make you more dangerous in some capacity.

Imagine the gladiators or Spartans or the Marines training. They train for something useful, combat. Not to look good in a mirror. That is how you should approach your training. Always include some sort of combat focus in your training, so not using weights alone as great as they can be. Make sure to include a martial art of some sort. Boxing, grappling, military combat, jiu-jitsu, I don't care but whatever it is train to get better at it.

Not to achieve simple proficiency but to excel.

Summary

Cultivate the skill to fight and more importantly the will to fight. Without the will the body is useless. With the will much can be accomplished. Things are returning to survival of the fittest and if you are a law abiding hard working citizen then you are going to be a target for the barbarians and those at the top. The only way to be safe is to the baddest barbarian there is. Which isn't always possible but at the very least you can help yourself by not being a soft target.

Remember criminals often operate as predators looking for the weak to pick on. They operate like bullies. They don't take on the football captain who also boxes and has an anger problem. No, they pick on those that they can. Don't be one of those that they can. Become dangerous and walk with confidence that you can handle yourself should violence arise. Be dangerous, be a man.

Prey, Predators, & Alpha Predators

Humans are animals. I don't mean this as an insult nor do I mean it as I'm about to step up on a high horse and tell us all how were supposed to be nice or whatever to others. I try to separate the information in this book from emotions, codes, and morality and simply present the facts. Not because I am against morality per se, simply that it can obscure truth. A prime example of this is the difference between a good man and a man who is good at being a man.

A good man is a man who does everything our society says he does. He's a good feminist, not racist, thinks homosexuality is the greatest thing since sliced bread, has no balls, etc. This is what it takes to be considered a good man by the government, societies, and churches (among others) in the Western world. Whereas a man who is good at being a man is a masculine man. He embraces his masculinity and all that comes with it. He is often hated by society as men are hard to control, real men that is, not castrated sheep.

Humans function in animalistic ways. You have alphas and betas.

You have fighting for dominance, resources, and survival. Don't get me wrong I'm not saying humans are simply animals, but that they have an animal nature that is shared with a thinking nature shared with that beyond animals. Humans have one foot on that above and one foot on that below occupying a middle plane. Like animals there are predators and prey. Regardless if you like it or not man is a violent creature. One that will prey on destroy the weak and feeble if given the chance. Factor in race, cultural, or religious differences and this desire increases tenfold.

To survive is the world you must become an alpha predator. The suburb gates will only hold back the tide so long. You live in a changing world. Where your political views can get you jumped, the color of your skin can have you killed, and the state will laugh as they shoot you in the back. You cannot afford to be weak in this world, never have and never will. You must have the will to fight. The world is divided into three categories of men (with all women and children being in the prey category). Which will be explained below.

Prey

This makes up the vast majority of the populace. These are docile fools. The sheep who are easily preyed upon. These types of people generally have a disdain for anything related to violence and live sheltered lives. When things go south as they inevitably do these are the first people to die. These types of people often expect others to protect them or even think that they could never be exposed to violence. They live in bubbles and therefore can afford to have ideologies that don't match up with the reality of the world at all.

These are the people you hear in the news complaining about some law of nature and the real way the world is. Whether it's they whining about violence, guns, or war. These people think that peace is something that is maintained through diplomacy instead of through the threat of violence. They fail to understand that strength is the only way to get respect. That hurting the enemy worse than he can hurt you is the only way to avoid conflict. Prey is easy to spot. They are herd animals, following along blissfully ignorant of the reality that surrounds them, until it's too late.

Predators

These are the thugs, the bullies, the criminals, and the guerrillas.

They prey upon the prey. Dangerous in numbers and more than a match for the average member of the prey. They exploit weakness whenever they can. They get a kick out of being stronger than someone. In high school they were the kid picking on the nerds or the wimps. They generally run in packs with a head predator who may actually be in the category below. They have their power because they know they have a better capacity for violence than does the vast majority of prey.

They aren't necessarily strong it's just that their not piss weak. Again numbers are an essential part of their strategy. Numbers and lack of opposition. They're the ones in the old movies that would take over the town if the law was weak and no one else would stand against them. The ruffians and robbers of the medieval times. The thugs and gangsters of today. They're generally loud but not always. Alone unless in a very weak prey environment there not nearly as boisterous. Like I said before they get a good portion of their strength from the pack (though lack of opposition is another way).

Alpha Predators

These are the lions of the world. You can find them alone, part of a special unit requiring training and dedication, and the lowest of the alpha predators head of packs or gangs of predators. These are the men that make the predators shit their pants. I don't know if you've ever seen the face of a goon when he goes after what he expects to be prey only to find out they would be prey is higher on the food chain than he is. The look is priceless. These are the Spartans, the SS. Elite fighters that make short work of predators and prey if they so choose. These men are not messed with.

To survive in this world especially if you are the wrong demographic you must be an alpha predator and even then that may not be enough. To avoid being harassed and or beaten you must become powerful and dangerous. For example political violence has spiked against those supporting true right wing candidates. Most of the victims were prey. This isn't to say they deserved it or that this is acceptable, simply stating facts. Meanwhile bikers support the same candidate and yet don't run into the same trouble that the college students do. Because the bikers have more in common with the alpha predator than prey and the college students have more in common with prey than the alpha predators.

Summary

Things are only going downhill. With the social and demographical change no one will be sheltered for much longer (except perhaps politicians and the uber rich). Your suburban hideaways will fall and you will have to deal with the realities of that. The countryside's will be developed to make room for the invaders, so even rural living will not save you. The only thing that has the possibility to save you is becoming an alpha predator. Becoming strong and dominant.

Be an alpha predator. Learn useful martial arts, practice point shooting, become familiar with firearms and other weaponry.

Understand the mental aspect of violence. Be prepared. We may not have voted for this world but it is the world that is coming for us. Learn self-defense, it will be vital to surviving the future. Don't be a victim, be a man. Take the responsibility for your safety and yourself into your own hands.

The World Is Not Your Friend

Many would like to forget. But this world is a kill or get killed world. A eat or be eaten world. Those who believe otherwise have been lulled to sleep by sweet lies in order to make them easier prey when their time is up. I say fuck that shit. Don't be lulled to sleep. Stay awake, stay strong, stay alive. The world is not your friend. The world will tear you up, bend you over, and spit you out. If you seek comfort first in this world you will be destroyed. Only those who have achieved power can hope to have any measure of freedom and comfort.

This applies doubly when you stand against the current of the world. When you refuse to a weakened slave but instead strive to be a free man with principles you will become a target. It will be up to you to make it through. Unless you were incredibly lucky your parents, teachings, and just about everything else will be useless. It's going to be you against the world in a one on one match and if you haven't been training it'll crush you.

Kill Or Get Killed

Weak wolves don't last long, weak lions don't last long, neither do weak men. A wolf who can't rip the throat out of every wolf he meets will eventually get his throat ripped out. It's the way of the world, and it's not different with man. You are either prey, predator, or alpha predator. And this applies to all facets of your life. Work, dating, and of course survival. A boss that can toy with you and eventually crush you…will. Unless you can destroy him first. Weak males will get cheated on, left, and laughed out while women will flock to the strong.

Perhaps you can find some exceptions to this, but you would be foolish to base your life on exceptions. Not everyone who sticks their head in a gator's mouth loses it, does that make it a wise move? I don't say this to scare you or to whine about how "awful" the world is. I tell you this so you will be prepared. Just like a drill instructor put his troops through living hell not because he gets some sadistic pleasure from it or because he wants to see them suffer. No, he does it because he cares and he knows the living hell some of his troops will be exposed to and he needs them to be prepared to have any hope of survival.

We Are Harsh Because We Care

The more you sweat in training the less you bleed in war. And life is war. Don't expect mercy and don't expect fairness for there is none. There is only strength and weakness. There are those that do what they will because they have power and those that tolerate it because they have no power. Nothing more and nothing less. The only way to make it and the only way to accomplish anything (for good or for ill) is to be strong enough to stand on your own two feet and go toe to toe with whatever the world will throw at you.

You are living in enemy lands. You can't even rely on your family.

And doing so will get you killed. You must take responsibility for everything in your life. Unlike the wolf or lion you won't meet a swift death but rather lifelong servitude. To a corporation that is doing everything it can to make who you are extinct, to a wife who after cheating multiple times got the kids and your money, to someone attacking you in the street because there is no consequence for doing so. Only the strong can ensure this is not their fate.

Only The Strong Survive

Any good soldier will tell you not being aware of what is going on around you will get you killed.

Women and children can skimp by in life with their head in the clouds a man cannot. You must be aware of what is going on around you. The changes that could spell disaster for you if you don't get moving. Other men will be the only ones who will tell you this. Weak males will tell you otherwise (until they are destroyed and become bitter) as well as will women and children (because they can afford to think in such a way).

Again this isn't to scare you or say how horrible the world is. But you have to be prepared. You have to sharpen your survival skills. Just like if I was your tribes leader and told you not to worry about killing or warfare the only thing it would do is put you in shock when the enemy tribe invaded the village. I'd be a horrible leader and a traitor to you. Instead I want you to know what lurks out there and the only way to keep it in check is to be able to destroy it.

Summary

Look some can make it through life without being prepared but they are few and far in-between (talking about men). You have to ask yourself "Am I prepared?". If my boss cut me tomorrow am I prepared? If my wife/girlfriend/slam pieces all left me tomorrow am I prepared? If I was attacked upon walking out my door am I prepared? If you answer no the any of these questions then you know what you need to do…prepare.

Competition Isn't Optional

The Strongest Survive

Not exactly politically correct but it is the truth. And that is what matters, the truth.

Many people shy away from competition from a fight. This is a natural inclination as it is natural to seek the easier option. We are inherently lazy and this is something we must fight every day. The smoother and easier path will feel good in the moment but ultimately cause more pain in the end.

There are many examples of this I can think of. Masturbating to porn instead of going out and talking to women. Paying for something in installments instead of fronting the cash. Lying in bed for that extra thirty or so minutes instead of getting up and hitting the gym. Watching TV instead of sitting down and reading a chapter out of a book. Mindlessly surf social media instead of writing up your next blog post or working on your book.

The examples are literally endless and they all have one theme in common. Taking the easier wrong over the harder right. Instant gratification over delayed. Taking the penny now over the dollar tomorrow.

Doing this before had instant consequences. You didn't hunt, you then starved to death. You got out of shape, you were soon picked off.

However we are now sheltered from the Darwinian system of survival. Yet the rules are still in effect. Get fat, emasculated, and lazy and it's only a matter of time before your girlfriend is picked up by someone who isn't fat, emasculated, and lazy. Unless of course she becomes fat, masculine, and lazy.

Competition is still in effect and because of this we must work hard every day to ensure that we are able to weather what the future holds.

Competition is King

Competition is great. Competition though looked down on in our society of sheep is essential to a man's development. To fight and sharpen yourself against other men to come out bigger, faster, stronger, smarter, and more. Like it says in the Bible "As iron sharpens iron, so one man sharpens another".

For those of who you may not have men to compete against in your life you're not excused. You're never excused. The greatest competition will be with yourself. To be better than you were yesterday. It is a relentless never ending competition. One that can be the most rewarding.

Never shy away from competition, from a fight. Embrace every opportunity to put your nuts on the line and go for it. Embrace the fighting spirit. The warrior that resides deep inside of you. That resides deep inside of every man. Society will try to get you to shun it but you must fight against that programming and embrace it.

Competition is a gift. A gift from God for the betterment of man.

The Illusion of Comfort

Comfort…is a lie.

Most humans seek comfort. It is a natural inclination. However in today's world it will constantly elude you or even once achieved may be taken away at any time.

Comfort is what makes the middle-class. The disappearing middle-class. Most do not strive for riches or for greatness. They are content with just getting by. With having "enough" Unfortunately when the tides turn against them, as they are. They will soon find that their comfort was a lie. That their assurance of the life they were promised will be taken from them.

The rich will not have this problem because they went higher.

They went after growth, success, to be the best instead of being "okay" or having "enough". Only the rich can hope to have what the middle-class believes they have and even then nothing is guaranteed.

So What Does This Mean?

It means be the best. It means fight the good fight and never back down. It means embrace competition as the gift that it is. Let it invigorate your fighting spirit, your masculine spirit, your inner warrior. Don't accept being a loser or even worse being "average".

Strive, fight, win.

The opposite of great is not bad. There are plenty of people who have come up from nothing. The desperate have the drive, the hunger, the fight. They know that there is much work to be done. On themselves and on their dreams. They know that competition is always there and that it can be used to better themselves. It is the middle, the good as opposed to great that have the most to worry about. They sit back because they think they are better than the bad. They look down when they should be looking up. Don't get me wrong there are rich and poor people with this mentality. It just that being good at something usually hinders greatness more than sucking at something.

Remember you cannot run from competition and nor should you. Embrace it and strive to become the best that you can be. That is the only true path that will lead to fulfillment.

Dominance

Dominance. Perhaps more than any other trait it the fundamental trait that makes a man a man. Dominance is what allows a man to make his impression on the world. It allows him to control himself, others (especially women), and even the world around him. Dominant men shape the world to fit to their ideals and ideas, while passive males allow the world to shape them it's ideals.

Dominance is a, if not the, fundamental aspect of being a man. Embrace it, utilize it, and then direct it.

Men were created to shape the world to share in the act of creation, to be creators. This is something I discussed in The Primer but wish to delve deeper into another aspect here. Dominance automatically gets a response from others and the world around you. A man who displays dominance or who is dominant stands out to others and the world like a diamond in a sea of coal. A man who knows what he wants and goes after it. A man who imposes his will on reality changing reality to fit it. This man makes use of his mind and his masculinity and the world responds to that.

Men respect him even when they envy him. Women cannot resist him. And the universe becomes plastic to the molding powers of his thoughts and actions. Things do not happen to him he happens to things essentially. He is an action as well as a risk taker and so much more. I could spend all day listing the different traits that make up a dominant man but that is not the point of this chapter.

Dominance Over Himself

The first thing that a man must dominate is his own mind. Once he has his mind firmly under his own control and is directing it as he wishes, he can achieve just about anything that he wishes. Self-mastery is truly the greatest mastery of them all. When self-mastery is the fundamental basis from which you work you will be successful in your ventures. Men who have mastered themselves have a much easier time mastering others and shaping reality to their ideals.

The first step in dominance is to take control of your mind and adapt the correct mindset. When this is done everything else begins to fall in place. Take control of your thoughts and harness the great power of your mind to get it working for you instead of against you. This is not a step that can be skipped or glossed over. It is the foundation, it is what everything else rests upon. Without this you will be like the builder who built his house upon the sand and when the rains came…well you know the rest.

Master your mind and be the man who built his house upon the rock and when the rains came he didn't give a damn because he built his house upon rock.

Dominance Over Others

Once a man has mastered himself he can then work on domination in relation to others. When most people think about being dominant in relation to others. They think of a domineering loudmouthed asshole which is not at all what I am getting at here. Domineering loudmouth assholes are little boys who are overcompensating for something. No, a dominant man can be quiet and often nice (unless you cross him). He may walk around not drawing attention to himself but there is something there that is undeniable and powerful. A primal energy that people just know. Dominance is to being domineering what confidence is to arrogance. One is healthy, essential, and attractive the other stems from insecurities and is seen through.

There is no force on this earth that women respond stronger to than dominance. Dominance is like catnip for women. Again remember this isn't being domineering. Men who always are fighting and yelling at their woman are insecure little boys not the dominant man we are talking about. A man who is dominant in control of both himself and his reality will be irresistible to women. It's not something that they can choose to be attracted to or not, they simply are. Like a woman with a nice round ass and a skinny waist as a man you have no choice whether you are attracted to her or not, you simply are. While looks are what men look for in women, dominance is what women look for in men as far as mating goes.

Dominance Over Reality

Reality can be molded. The world is shaped by men who decided that they wanted to shape it. Life is not a passive journey where fates decide where you end up. If you are a man you have the power to shape the world around you into what you wish. Not necessarily the entire world (though that is possible) but your own world, the one that actually matters to you. You can create the life that you want and impose your will on reality. Like how God called matter out of nothing you can also call the life you want out of the life you have. As men were given the power to be co-creators (obviously on a much smaller scale but nevertheless).

Remember this all stems from dominance over your own mind. Once that is accomplished having dominance over others and over your world often naturally falls into place and even if not, it takes a little work to get it there. Men are called to be dominant. Over themselves, in their lives, in relation to women, and in relation to others. Men were created to be dominant. The world needs dominant men who will make a place worth living. It is men who shape the world but first taking control of themselves.

Why Weakness Has No Part In A Man's Life

Man and women are different. Not just by a little but fundamentally. Like fire and ice. This fact while not approved by our Frankenstein society has held true since the inception of man and will hold true until his extinction. One of the prime differences is as I said in The Primer

"Becoming a man is a process, while a girl may mature into a women simply by biologically aging it is not the same with men. Many males die still boys, even if their biological age may be one hundred."

Girls naturally mature into women they don't have to do anything to do so. However with a man he must be initiated into manhood by other men. A woman cannot turn a boy into a man, ever. Doesn't matter how good her intentions are or how loving, caring, or whatever a woman is. It is biologically impossible for a woman to raise a boy into a man. Hence so many issues with boys (well and girls but that's a different story) raised by single mothers. They simply are not biologically equipped to do so.

Weakness

A man will die if he is weak. Perhaps not physically (anymore) but spiritually and mentally. Weakness runs antithetical to masculinity. Despite what modern "men's" movements will say about how embracing weakness and admitting one's faults is the way to masculinity they are wrong. Admitting one's faults does nothing and embracing weakness is disgusting. One should seek to ruthlessly eliminate one's faults simply admitting them will do you no good.

Admitting to a circle of men that you have a particular weakness while it may feel good in the moment will do nothing for you in the long term. Only by identifying and then fighting tooth and nail against the weakness will you improve and better yourself. Weakness has no place in a man's life and that includes weakness of any kind. Physically, mentally, and spiritually. A man must have a strong will that he uses to shape the world around him, that he uses to shape the very fabric of reality.

No Mercy

Many have griped about how women get special treatment. For example when a girl hurts herself she is generally coddled and allowed to sit out meanwhile when a boy hurts himself he is told to rub dirt in it or man up and then required to continue what he is doing. This is how it should be. This is the natural order. MRA's, the "men's" movement, and Feminist's would have you believe in an unnatural order where all are equal. A order that has never existed and will never exist. A order when tried to be enforced results in destruction of society and suffering for the individuals in that society.

The world will not show a man mercy and he should not show the world mercy either. A man must thrust himself upon the world and subdue it, same with a woman. Women have no respect and even disdain for weak men. They may not admit it but weak men repulse them as weak men repulse the world. When you were born with a dick you were born with to either fully become a man or to sink to the bottom. Women may be able to exist at a mid-level but men do not have that choice. They either ascend and conquer or regress and are defeated.

The Choice

The choice is yours what you will do. Will you grab life by the horns and become a man? Or will you retreat from the struggle and forever remain a little boy? There is no other option, you are not a woman, for you it is either victory or defeat. Conquer or be conquered. Because you are male and this is the way of the world. You can retreat adopting ideologies that run against nature or you can stand and reassert the natural order. It is your choice, it is up to you.

Your choice and the choice of the males around you is going to decide the future. Women simply react it is men who create it is men who shape. It is men who have the power to change society to change reality, should they choose to use it. Never forget the famous words of Edmund Burke

"The only thing necessary for the triumph of evil is that good men do nothing"

Men not women, but men. There is plenty of evil in our society no doubt about it. Up is being called down, wrong right, and true false. The natural order is being replaced by a Frankenstein order that will destroy us all if we let it. Also good men not nice men but good men. Men who are good at being men as Jack Donovan would say.

The Will To Fight

Outnumbered, outgunned, surrounded with no hope of survival.

Death surrounding you, consuming you, numbness gripping you.

You mind focused like a laser on survival.

The only thing you have is what is inside you. Fists, knives, weapons merely extensions of the will within, of your mind. Tools.

Tools that are useless without the fighting spirit within you.

Men have risen above situations such as the ones described above.

These men understand violence and the will.

Violence, something that seems so far away from so many people yet is a fundamental part of the natural order. A fundamental part of life and the operation of the universe.

"Violence is never an option" can only be said by insulated pussies who have been sheltered and protected their entire lives from reality. By men who use violence.

A man who won't fight isn't a man, he cannot be. The will to fight is what breathes life into the masculine spirit. It's what animates a man's heart and inflames his passion.

Embracing the Warrior

People love to hear stories of the ancient Greek heroes. Even in our corrupt modern cinema we still have movies about the heroism of man against great odds. The story of the Spartans standing against the Persian hordes still lights something in the hearts of men across the globe. There is something deep inside man that is aware of the hostility of nature. Of the fierce competition and fight that underlies existence. The volcano of human nature that bubbles underneath the thin veneer of civilization.

A male who cannot embrace his warrior side and embrace violence isn't a man. His function has been corrupted by society, religion, or some other cancerous growth. This isn't to say religion or society in and of themselves are cancerous simply much of their modern manifestations are. Nor am I saying to love violence for the sake of violence. Simply saying to accept the need for it and the reality of it.

Push a man and he can use his words but ultimately words are cheap. Action is what separates men from the rest. A male who won't fight, who won't inflict violence will always be kicked and pushed around. He will be a slave for he has embraced a slave nature, women will resent him, children will have no respect for him, and other men will do with him as they please. The will to fight is how a man asserts himself into the world and claims his rightful place as king of nature, as man.

Worse Than Death

Survival is a deeply ingrained need. However throughout the ages there are many things that men have valued more than survival. Namely honor and pride. Two things all men have in themselves. Nowadays males will sacrifice their dignity for a few bucks or even worse the approval of women or society. They have lost this spirit and because of this have lost what makes them a man. They have lost their very essence.

Losing your manhood is worse than death. Throughout the ages man has known this, man has understood this. Man has understood that life while good is not the end all be all. Nowadays especially with the decline in people who believe in something greater, people hold onto their survival and comfort over everything. Sure I'll bow down and you can give to me hard just please don't make me do something uncomfortable. The quote of the modern male.

Lying down simply increases the pain. Only by fighting can things be solved. Only by fighting can things get better. A male who is weak is hated by all. One belief that has given men strength is the belief that there is an afterlife and they will be judged for their behavior. I personally believe that this life is simply a stepping stone and that what we call the spirit or soul lives on while the physical body ceases to function. I also believe that I will sit down before my creator and be judged for my actions. And if I don't measure up I will be as Conan would say "cast out of Valhalla as he laughs at me". You don't have to share my beliefs but regardless you must keep yourself from the consumerism and narcissism of this age. The pointless mental masturbation that goes on. Understand there is something deeper and cut yourself from vain sources. Focus on what is good.

In The End

In the end there is only you and your manhood. Live a life worth living, live a life filled with pride and vigor. Embrace your masculinity and your fighting spirit. Honor your creator by being what you were created to be not what society would have you be. Be a shining light in the darkness. A healthy being in a cancerous age. A man among males. Your creator will smile upon you, nature will give to you, women and children will follow and respect you. Because you have fulfilled what you were created to be. Embrace the fighting nature and understand that violence is the reality of this world. Have the will to fight.

Being Unapologetic: A Key Tenet Of Masculinity

One of the most lacking traits of masculinity in our culture is being unapologetic. We've been trained to apologize for everything that happens. Males are made to be like Pavlov's dogs to respond to everything with an apology. We have been taught that being apologetic is a virtue of some kind. That to be apologetic makes us "noble" or "good" in some way, shape, or form.

However the truth is being apologetic is no virtue and more often than not more an offense than anything. An offense against your masculinity and balls. The worst kind of offense. It's not that apologizing in and of itself is evil, simply that it has been hijacked to make you a slave to what society wants. There are some things you should never apologize for. Namely your heritage, your masculinity, and your personal desires.

Your Heritage

I don't give a damn who you are, you should be proud of your ancestors and your heritage. You should honor them and strive to further their legacy. A male who hates on his ancestors is disgusting. Especially when it's to appease those that hate him. Like I said before weakness has no part in a man's life. Never apologize for your ancestors and for your blood. You blood is a part of you just like your balls are. You must embrace every part of yourself. This includes your ancestry. Society benefits from a man being separated from his bloodline and heritage as it makes him easier to marginalize and manipulate.

Be proud of who you are. You are who you are for a reason. Never let anyone, and I mean anyone convince you to be ashamed of your ancestry and heritage. Never apologize for your ancestors. Make them proud. Don't let others shame or guilt you into surrendering your balls. Stand strong and be a man. Be proud of your heritage. In others word be unapologetic for your heritage.

Your Masculinity

Another thing that society will try to shame you for is being a man. It has all but been made illegal to have balls in Western society. The media, government, schools, and just about everything else constantly harps on how evil/bad/awful masculinity is and men are. Nearly every problem is blamed on men. Women are given the go ahead to do as they please while men and masculinity are opposed at every turn. Put simply modern society hates masculinity. The reason being men (meaning masculine men) are the only ones who can throw a monkey wrench into the whole corrupt system bringing it crashing down and ushering in a new age of freedom, but that's a topic for another time.

A man who embraces his masculinity is a rare find a man who embraces his masculinity and makes no apologies for is the rarest of finds. Be a man like this. When someone tries to shame you for your masculinity tell them either to fuck off or shrug your shoulders. The point is you aren't changing for anyone especially for some punk who wants to drink the same cool aid that they are. A male who won't bend to the will of others will stand out in the best way possible. Because he will be a man.

Your Desires

"You don't want to get married?", "You like young girls?", "You think woman should submit to men?" I've heard all of these said before generally in very accusatory tones yet never have I apologized for one view that I hold (and never will

I). When I held the frame those that shot these accusatory words generally left with smiles on their faces. Because like I said before they encountered one of the rarest creatures in Western civilization, a man. Never apologize for your desires or let others convince you that your desires are wrong. You're a man hold the frame and be unapologetic.

You see when you don't give in to the reality of others but stay true to your own, you do a couple of very important things. One you establish yourself as the dominant reality (as you always should), two you show that you have balls (which women love and men respect), and three you show that you stand by your convictions. Put simply you don't change for others and you unapologetic for who you are.

Remember

Being unapologetic is a key tenet of masculinity and one you should embody in all that you do. Take a unapologetic attitude toward life and fully embrace who and what you are. That includes your heritage, your masculinity, and your desires. Don't let society or others change you from your path. Be who you are, be a man. Unapologetically, fully a man.

On The Appeal Of The Outlaw

The Japanese have their samurai, the Europeans their knights, all cultures have a mythic past of warriors that they make up much of their stories. Men who young boys grow up wanting to be like and young girls grow up wanting to be with. Despite the modern whitewashing of most of these heroes, what appeals to everyone is a few key traits that make up a mythic class of warrior. Societies need heroes to function and fortunately people are going to respond to their biological functions in regards to what they admire.

No matter what a man (and a woman even if she doesn't admit it) is going to admire Leonidas or Jesse James more than some panty waste social justice warrior or just generally all around pussy. In America we have our outlaws. The wild west gunslinger. The kind Clint Eastwood or John Wayne would play. A man. Sometimes good and sometimes bad by societies standards but always a man. Meaning he may not be moral but he is masculine and that is what people admire (and frankly need).

There are many reasons that Americans always have and always will admire their outlaws. The outlaw represents something timeless and heroic. Something rugged and masculine. Something that resonated deep within every man's soul. These are the reasons the outlaw and heroes of all cultures appeal to us today (as they should).

Own Man

The outlaw is in control of his destiny and his life. Throw whatever hardships you may at him, he will have control. He is his own man. He doesn't answer to anyone except for himself. He has independence and freedom too things that all men desire. When he wakes up in the morning he doesn't answer to another power. Whether that power be a woman, a job, or the government.

The outlaw is in control. Something that cubicle slaves of the world have forgotten what it even feels like to have. Not only control but freedom. He may not be rich (doesn't stop women from adoring him of course) but he is free. He values freedom over comforts. He realizes that comfort can often lead to slavery so chooses a path more fitting for a man. A harder path yet a path of freedom.

Dangerous

The outlaw is a dangerous man. Society realizes on a primal level the appeal of a man who is capable of violence. This has held true since the inception of man and doesn't change just because man has moved into the suburbs. Being dangerous is an essential part of being a man. It's the only way to get respect. Men respect a man who has the capacity for violence and women are turned on by it.

Western males have become weak. They need to reclaim their masculinity. Assert their dominance and purge themselves of all weakness. They need to reclaim their heritage. Stop taking so much shit and be men. Another aspect of the outlaw that appeals to people is his assertion of his will. He doesn't take shit from anyone. Could you imagine a boss or a woman demeaning Jesse James or Bill The Kid without getting shot or at least smacked around? This because these men were men, real men. Just like the knights and the samurai and that is why they appeal so deeply across all levels of society. Because men appeal across all levels of society (even if that society says men and masculinity is evil). Remember biology trumps social delusions.

Masculinity

Outlaws are masculine and they make no apologies for it. They fully embrace their masculinity and everything that it entails. They don't let others shame them for it or for anything else. They do as they will and anyone who doesn't like it can go fuck themselves. Combine the embracing of their masculinity with a devil may care attitude and you have a potent combination.

Fear of death hampers most people in life. Everyone dies, and worrying about it will never do you any good. Heroes seem to have little fear of death instead focusing on living a life worth living. Living life to the fullest and making the most out of every moment. Whether it's to be remembered in the history books, to stand proud before their God, or just because that's how they are. They embrace a devil may care attitude.

Summary

Society is desperate for masculinity and men who embrace it. Men who do are remembered and honored throughout time, even centuries later. Nothing makes a larger impact than a masculine man. On society, on women, on children, on anything. Their impact echoes throughout time. Be a man who's legacy will echo throughout time. Be like the outlaw.

There Is No Competition For Masculine Men

Imagine you are looking at a herd of sheep grazing in a field. They're all relatively the same size, shape, and demeanor. Now say in that herd of sheep you see a lion. A male in his prime lion. Now let's say for whatever reason the lion doesn't kill all the sheep but lives among them. When you see the herd coming what is the first thing that you are going to notice? The lion obviously. Now let's say you're looking for an animal for fighting in a ring and a farmer takes you to the herd. Which one are you going to choose? Again the lion obviously.

Now say this herd for whatever reason decided to run a society. Who is going to be at the top of that society? Again the lion. I've got a point here so bear with me. In today's society more than anything else there is a lack of masculinity. A masculine man will stand out like a lion in a herd of sheep. A masculine man does not go unnoticed. By other men, by children, and especially by women. A masculine man has an impact wherever he goes simply by virtue of being masculine. When you embrace your masculinity and become a masculine man you put yourself so far above the pack that there is little to no competition. Like a lion competing among sheep.

In Leadership

Men are leaders and thereby the more masculine that a man is the more people will want to follow him. Also the more masculine a man is the more effective leader he will be, notice that I said effective not moral. A masculine leader will get things done for better of for worse. The conquerors of old whether Alexander the Great of Genghis Khan were both effective and masculine leaders. A man simply needs to assert himself and he will have the reigns given over to him, if not thrown over.

All defer to the most dominant and masculine man. Human beings though higher than the animals still have animalistic functions, one of which is the way we organize socially and establish hierarchies. I wrote about the sexual hierarchy before but the pyramid can be applied to more than just sexuality. It functions in tribal relations, between a hierarchy of friends, in business, in simple social interactions. It permeates everything.

With Women

Women are naturally attracted to masculinity, it's biological. Even the vast majority of lesbians (excluding bull dykes) cannot resist the allure of a masculine man. Women will leave their husbands, children, religions or anything simply to get a whiff of a masculine man. It's like a drug to women. A drug that is in very low supply. Be a masculine man and you'll have women throwing themselves at you left and right, it's inevitable.

Like a lion fighting a sheep, there just isn't even a contest there. That's how it is with a masculine man entering today's dating market.

A man who embraces his masculinity and his masculine dominance will have women falling at his feet. Masculinity (and all that it entails) does the same to women that a tight waist, large breasts, and a round ass with clear skin does to a man. It causes a reaction in him that he cannot control or resist. Double this for women and masculinity and you'll start to get the picture.

What Does This Mean For Me?

What this means is that though society may stand against you embracing your masculinity and call you evil or bad for doing so. The fact of the matter is there is not much better that you can do to live a greater life. Embracing your masculinity is the start of the process of getting the life that you want. A man who has distanced himself from his masculinity will never be happy. Like an eagle trapped in a cage. It's soul will cry out until it gets freedom or dies. The same is true with the soul of a man. It will cry out for its masculinity or it will die.

Feed your soul and embrace your masculinity. Become a masculine man. Become the man that you were created to be. If you never embrace your masculinity, you can never be fulfilled. You will go through life half alive at best. Embracing your masculinity is like shooting color into the eyes of someone who has only seen black and white their entire life. That and remember there is no competition for masculine men.

When Being Good Is Wrong

We lived in an upside down world, in a cancerous society. The values that held together society and civilization for the past thousands of years and longer have been replaced with "values" that make us sheep to the slaughter, that enslave us. Yet day in and day out we are taught to be good, to be well behaved. Any man who might get in the way of the scheme of how things are headed is declared "bad", "evil", or (insert "ist/phobic" here).

In today's world sheep are declared to be paragons of virtue and it makes sense. When wolves rule the rules are used to make fatter, tastier, and dumber sheep. The rules are used against us. Throw out their rules and create your own. Being good is wrong. Being bad is right. At least according to our modern society. Embrace your "bad" side, embrace your masculinity, embrace who you are.

Good Is Wrong

To be good in today's society there are some rules that you must follow. A key one is you must be completely balless. You have to go along with whatever the media and government says is good with a smile on your face. You must do whatever your wife wants, no matter how asinine it is. You must be tolerant if all even it you know it's perverted or those who you are supposed to tolerate hate your guts. You must apologize for your ancestors and for being born with a Y chromosome. Essentially you must bend over and take it while smiling saying thank you sir may I have another.

The meaning of the word "good" has been hijacked. Along with many others as after all language has incredible power to change a society. For example to be a "good man" you must essentially be a castrated wimp who agrees with whatever his Feminist overlord wants. Think I'm kidding google the good man project. Have a Conan movie or Manowar song queued up to purge your eyes and mind afterwards. Essentially being good is wrong in our modern world and something that every man should avoid.

Being Bad Is Right

So now we look at the other side of the coin. What is considered evil in our society? Believing men should be masculine and women should be feminine. Believing invading hordes do not add to the development of a country. Believing that the nuclear family is the best way to raise children. Not worshiping women. And so on and so forth. Essentially everything that makes for healthy men, women, and society is considered bad or evil.

Being declared a bad man by society is a badge of honor and means you are doing something right. Look at it like this in a healthy group being declared honorably by that group is in fact honorably. Likewise in an unhealthy group being declared honorable is an insult.

Look at the Nobel peace prize at one time that prize meant something. Now it's turned into a politically correct circle jerk. Same with pretty much any major awards given in American society. How much longer before a soldier is given the Medal of Honor for being gay or transgender or whatever mental disorder becomes popular? Now to receive the Nobel peace prize is a joke and everyone knows it.

What This Means For You

Screw being good, embrace that society will be against you. Be an outlaw, at least until society rights itself and even then who knows you might not want to go back. There is power in freedom. Do what you know to be right and go against societies rules if they conflict with what you believe to be right. At one point society, religion, schools, etc. could be used as guiding lights for our path but not anymore. Now a man must forge his own path with like-minded men. Men who shun weakness and slavery. Men who still have their balls and hearts intact. Good is wrong. Bad is right. Embrace being bad.

Claim Your Destiny

Nothing can stand in the way of one who is focused. Nothing can stay in the way of a man who has claimed his masculinity and knows his task before him. No government, no outside force, can stand in the way of a man who has harness that which is inside him and set it in motion. Kingdoms have been undone by single men, wars have been won by single men, the fate of the world has been changed by single men.

Give me a man dedicated to his cause and he will beat back one hundred men who are not. The man who has taken possession of his will and duty is unstoppable. Combine this with the will to fight and a man becomes the most powerful force there is on this earth. Man was created to be powerful, to be strong, to be man. Our culture has turned this into a parody. Either man as evil or man as castrated loser. When to be a man is the highest calling that there is.

Power

Something I hate about many anti-feminist movements despite the good things that they do is how they label men as powerless. As weak and victims. While I get what they are getting at they are doing men a disservice by blinding men to the power that they are capable of. They are clipping the wings of potential eagles. Men are powerful when they embrace their masculinity and throw off the shackles of a corrupted and decadent society. There is nothing masculine or empowering about whining or bitching as men do not whine or bitch but get things done. They either put up or shut up.

Instead of whining about legislation not being passed for men (since when have men given a fuck about laws?) instead they should be focusing on being men and the women and society will adjust themselves accordingly. Because they will have no other option.

Because what men want is what happens, which is why governments struggle so hard to castrate men. They are a threat to their power because they are in fact powerful. A bear is not threatened by a limp camel but will look twice at a lion.

The Threat

Because men represent a threat to the NWO or any order that seeks to enslave the masses for their own schemes, men and masculinity are essentially outlawed. Men are told that masculinity is evil or that masculinity consists of working out at the gym or drinking beers. When masculinity is a deep, visceral, primal, and ethereal thing. It covers all facets of life. It is life giving and life taking. It is creative and destructive. Masculinity mirrors God himself as femininity mirrors God's creation, nature.

This is a threat to the enemy and they know it. To be a man in a world that is doing everything it can day and night to eradicate manhood is an accomplishment. Manhood has been lying in the dust long forgotten. It needs to be risen from the sands and placed at the head of the kingdom. It needs to reclaim it's rightful place as head. Just as God is the head over creation. Man the head over woman. So is masculinity the headship over the society.

Rise Up

Rise up, claim your mantle, become a king, and join the masculine rising across the world. You cannot hold a power down that guide created to be head of creation for long. It will come back and when it does it will rise like the phoenix. There will be a cleansing and then a restoration of all that is good and noble. Be part of this special time in history. Claim your destiny to be remembered in the history books and before your God. If you are a man then you were created to be a champion. Not a whiner or loser. You were created to accomplish great things. All men are but few ever embrace it.

To be a man is to given the opportunity to be most like God than any other creation other than the angels. When you look at the history books as well as the religious texts over the world in the end it is the right order that prevails. This unholy Babylon we have over us only lasts so long before it is destroyed. It's cracks are beginning to show. A rebellion for good is around the corner. The world is getting ready to right itself once more. Masculine men are growing by the day and feminine women will soon be following them. The hydra can be slain the dragon defeated, but it must be done by a man. Are you ready to embrace your destiny, achieve greatness, and take your ranks among men and claim your destiny.

Lay Claim To The Earth

As men we have a unique place in creation. We were created to mirror the power of the creator, something not given to any other facet of creation. Not the animals, not nature, and not women. We were uniquely given that. We were created to be lord over creation. A gift that we have tossed aside. We had traded in our crowns for chains. We have given up the throne to a poisonous system and mindset. We have let the darkness shut out the light and now the world suffers for it.

But there is a resurgence. There is a faint light in the darkness. Masculinity though opposed on all fronts by government, society, religion, and more has not faded and there is still a small flicker that has the capacity to become so much more. One man with his balls and soul intact can turn away one hundred that have lost theirs and in are in chains to their overlords. Samson with the jawbone of a donkey killed a thousand men. As the great American Andrew Jackson once said "One man with courage makes a majority". One man with the will of iron will crush thousands if not millions with wills of paper.

However even with the great birthright that comes with being a man it means nothing if we do not embrace it. Our birthright is useless if we toss it aside or do nothing with it. The crown is there if we are willing to take it, the earth is ours if we would but reach out and take it. You were born to be a king. To be a king you must not back down, you must not apologize. You must go forth and conquer as you born to do. Reclaim the land from all that has corrupted it. You are man, you have been given power. However you must use it.

A Man Goes After What He Wants

A man goes directly after what he wants. He doesn't ask permission, he doesn't wait for the go ahead, he simply goes. He does not wait around for anyone or anything. He sees, he goes, he conquers. That is man. He sees a job he wants he goes for it, a woman he wants he goes after it. He doesn't sit around and hope for the best, a man takes action. Action is part of being a man. While women and children can survive passively, a man cannot. A man must be a man of action, there is no other kind.

A man listens to his own heart and goes his own way. He forges his own path outside the boundaries of others. He goes by his own code and is respected and sometimes feared for it. He doesn't bow to social pressure but only by what comes from within. He cannot be guilted or shamed for what he wants as the opinions of others mean nothing to him. A man operates outside the constrains of society, it's the only way to keep his manhood and therefore soul intact. This doesn't mean he is necessarily a wander or loner, he can still live and operate in society without being controlled by it. He is in the world but not of it. Nor does this mean he is a lawbreaker but rather that he walks his own way.

A Man Takes What He Wants

Like I said above a man does not ask for permission. He is his own permission. He is his own force of action. He doesn't need anything outside himself. The laws of his society while he understand them do not confine him. He does not become a slave to the social contract that society would force upon him. He doesn't follow the rules lain out for him but forged his own code that he lives by. When a man sees something that he wants he takes it.

No second thoughts, no doubts. He sees what it is he wants, he takes it, and destroys anything that is foolish enough to get in his way. He takes what he wants without apology or remorse. If others don't like it too damn bad that isn't his problem. A man understands that to get what you want out of this life and world that you must take it. Nothing is going to be given to you. You the man must go after it. You as a man are the active force and everything else in the world the passive.

A Man Claims What Is His

A man understands that he is at the top of the food chain. He understands the concept of ownership. He is not afraid to assert that ownership either. He does not let others walk over him or push him around. He takes a firm stand and any who try to move him will fail. The only thing that can move him is his own heart and soul. His compass upon which he leans for his direction in life. A man has the will to fight. When someone disputes his claim he asserts it even harder.

He does not let others take that which is his and he will do what is necessary to prove that point. You cannot take something from a man that he doesn't want taken without a fight. He lays claim to that he wants. He doesn't care what others think or say about it. Because it is his own heart, soul, and will that he is following and asserting not the heart, soul, and will of another or others. A man follows his own path and stakes his claim on the earth and all that is in it.

Summary

You should recognize a common theme here. Being impervious to the will of others while asserting one's will. Again

Being impervious to the will of others while unapolgetically asserting one's own will.

Weak men, women, and governments/religions will call this evil and selfish. They call it this because it takes away the power they have over men and puts it back where it belongs. Into the hands of the man himself. Men are used as slaves for women and those who control society. They are also the only thing that can bring the whole thing down. Like Samson brought the temple down upon the philistines. Don't let them chain you down, don't let them cut your hair in the first place. Be free and true to yourself as a man and die with you masculinity intact and your soul still fully alive. So that when you pass into the next world you can do so with a smile on your face and pride in your heart.

Again this does not mean a man breaks the law as that would be foolish. Rather he doesn't follow the "unofficial" rules that society has lain out for him. For example he'll take a business deal because he wants it, he'll approach a hot girl because he thinks she is attractive, and so on and so forth.

Why Weak Men Hate & Fear Strong Men

Weak men fear strong men. This shows itself time and time again in a myriad of ways. From politics to sports to things that matter. The weak man since time immemorial has done all that he can to throw chains on the strong man and suppress him. Yeah it's not quite a one street like they would have you believe. The weak has always gathered together to take down the strong. So when the strong dispatched the weak it was never done with remorse as they knew the weak would do the exact same to them if they were given the chance. I'm not talking about physical weakness necessarily (though that plays a part) I'm talking about the strength and weakness of a man's heart and soul, his balls in other words.

Hell most religions and governments are geared around oppressing the strong man in favor of the weak. Look at one of the worst governing systems there is democracy. Where the lowest common denominator drowns out everything else. The Wal-Mart of political ideologies. Yet the masses love such an ideology because it makes their weakness an asset instead of a liability, as nature intended it to be. For example being a sniveling backstabber would get you head pounded in eons (or twenty years) ago. Now being a sniveling cuck is a badge of honor in our society. But I'm getting sidetracked back to the topic at hand.

Why The Weak Hate The Strong

You've seen it before. To their face the weak masses won't say shit to a man yet behind his back conspire against him and work in underhand ways against him, like women. I've seen this firsthand. A guy who has his balls in tact is like catnip for women so women naturally respond to me in a strong primal way. This pisses off weak men as to them I'm a "misogynist, homophobic, evil, awful, asshole" and while I can't argue with the last label they are projecting their hatred because they aren't me. They see the way women, including their sisters, friends, girlfriends, wives, mothers, and pretty much every other female responds to me and they hate it, because they're not it.

Now a man who isn't good at something will bust his ass to improve. For example say I got my ass whipped in boxing (which I have) what do I do in response? Do I go around and tell everyone how he's actually a shitty boxer or that he cheated or some other B.S. no I hit the gym and the bag twice as hard. If anything I congratulate the man for being skilled enough to beat me. Then I go to work to annihilate him should we meet again. That's how strong men handle things.

300

I remember when the movie 300 came out. I loved the movie. The fighting, the honor, the not surrendering, the unapologetic masculinity. Then I saw the response to it. For example I remember in history class my history teaching going on and on about how it was "historically inaccurate" and so on and so forth. As if that has ever mattered to Hollywood. I then saw others come out against it for this reason on that. Yet the reason they threw out for not liking that movie somehow didn't apply to other movies. It was violent yet they loved Pulp Fiction, it was historically inaccurate yet they loved Glory, you get the picture.

No it was something deeper that they feared and hated about the movie. It was the unapologetic masculine strength. Especially white unapologetic masculine strength which made it even more evil in the eyes of the weak masses of sheep. The weak males hate it because they can never be it. They women hated it because women go along with whatever the current social narrative is. And so on and so forth. They reason they hated it was because it showed how weak and incompetent they were. Like when yuppie college boys used to go and spit on soldiers. When they look in a face of a man they are reflected back them own weakness and deficiency. And as we know weakness has no part in a man's life.

Envy

It stems from envy. For example want to know how to identify someone who will always be poor? Their hatred of rich people.

You want to identify someone who will always be a loser? They hate the successful. Want to identify someone who will always be a pussy? They hate men with balls. And so on and so forth. Their hatred shows their own lack and what they will never be.

Look at the masses who are so eager to tear down Western civilization. Why is this? Because they know they could have never created it. Greatness strikes hated and anger into the inferior. They can't be those things so they must tear them down and destroy them so that they are not constantly reminded of their own inferiority.

Like Feminists who must destroy all feminine beauty, cucks who must destroy all masculinity and national pride.

Summary

There was a reason that the strong of before did not feel for the weak (of soul, not body). The reason being they were not worthy of care, mercy, or tolerance. Tolerance of evil is to be compliant to that evil. If you identified a cancer growth you wouldn't wait for it to grow before eliminating it. You would eliminate it right away. Now you understand why the weak hate you. Because of jealousy and envy. Entire political movements can be explained by this mental defect.

Be a man, stand strong in this world filled with weakness and depravity. Don't let the hatred of others control or change you. Stick to your path and become the best that you can be. The fear, envy, and jealousy of the sheep should be a signal to you that you are headed in the right direction. The fact that you can be bowed by social pressure will infuriate them more. Be a man and the world will fall at your feet.

How To Be A Modern Warrior Poet

The warrior poet. A man of both deeds and words. A man versed in both learning and combat. A man who makes the most out of himself. He develops his body to be dangerous and to be able to face the challenges that the world inevitably throws at men. Yet he also develops his mind making is stronger and broadening it beyond what he once thought possible. A man that knows how to use both the pen and the sword.

A man who does not fully develop all of his assets as a man can never fully be a man. A man can be strong but it will not be for much is he is a fool. Likewise a man can be intelligent but it will be for naught if he is a coward. A man must be both brave and wise. Strong and understanding. He must understand the ways of the world and mind and be able to face whatever threats that he may find out there.

Many males try to overcompensate for their lack of masculinity in a particular area. For example one kid who is naturally bigger will use that to take advantage of others kids. He will play up his size to the best of his ability. Likewise males with natural intelligence will do the opposite. They will use their wits to their advantage and maximize the use of those. However neither ever fully develop, they both remain in an perpetually adolescent state of existence and living. They never become men because they are only half men.

The Warrior Poet

The warrior poet like a man does not develop by inertia only by force of will. Becoming a man or a warrior poet is not something that "just happens". Things don't just happen for men, ever. Women sometimes but men never. A man must act his will out on the world and shape reality to it. The man is the active force. The only things he gets are those which he takes. He must go out and forge himself or he will be run over. There is no middle option for men. Either rise to the heights or sink to the depths, the middle ground exists only for women.

The warrior poet has spent time developing himself. It takes time to learn the ways of the world and the ways of violence. Of cultivating a love for knowledge as well as the will to fight. He develops all of his capacities to the best that he can. He doesn't let himself lean too much on a single thing as he knows that the world is dynamic and vicious in its testing. It will show no mercy to one who only has one set of skills. Violence, money, women, and more the world will throw them all at you. A man cannot hide he either faces the giant and emerges a victor or is crushed by it.

This idea of a middle path is often the death of a males quest to become a man. This idea of compromise and there being an easier way is nonsense. A man thrives or dies. He is not a passive force simply surviving. He is dynamic and active. He is either moving forward or moving backwards. Like I've said the feminine can stand still or follow the masculine but it is the masculine that must push forward. Like the old saying says "If it is up to be then it is up to me" men would do well to inscribe this motto on their heart and mind.

How To Become A Warrior Poet

So I've told you what a warrior poet is now an equally important question, how does one become one? What I do is point you in the right direction eventually you have to go your own path. But this is a good place to start. For apprentice warrior poets they must familiarize themselves with two things few males ever familiarize themselves with yet are crucial to their development as men and warrior poets. Those two things are violence and knowledge. If you are not reading at least a book and a week and spending at least five hours in combat or combat practice of some kind you are already failing.

Combat. Though I have my own preferred styles of combat the fact that you are struck and getting struck in a somewhat realistic manner is what matters. The on a nearly daily basis you are both receiving and inflicting pain. Again every day you are receiving pain and thereby learning to cope with it. And you are inflicting pain that you are also capable of dishing it out. You are familiarizing yourself with how two bodies act in combat situations. You are getting used to it, or as much as possible. So that when a violent confrontation happens in the real world you react on instinct.

Knowledge. A man without knowledge will not go far. Knowledge is power. Or at least applied knowledge is. Expanding your knowledge is one of the most important things that you can do. Knowledge gives you a leg up on everyone around you. It allows you to avoid pitfalls, leverage your time, and do just about anything. Knowledge is unlimited and will always have a higher ROI. Time spent reading a book, especially (but not limited too) a non-fiction one is nearly always time well spent. You are offered the world if you would just reach out and take it.

Summary

Set aside time to fight and read. Join a boxing gym or a dojo. Spent an hour every night before bed reading or perhaps an hour in the morning with a cup of tea. Whatever suits you the point is that you do it. Doing these two things will solidify your path to becoming a modern warrior poet and joining the ranks of the great men who came before you. Be a man of arms and letters, capable of facing anything. From the worst nature has to offer to the worst society has to offer. You will stand out head and shoulders above the crowd.

Without Freedom, We Have Nothing

This is not a chapter about politics, this about something far more important than politics. This about you and two of the most important things you can have. Your freedom and your masculinity. Which are linked together and can never be separated. Freedom, I think while it's a topic that isn't directly addressed often by men it is something that is often on men's minds. To be able to live the life that they want and how they see fit. To be able to follow their heart and develop themselves. To take the road that they want to take, that is freedom.

Freedom is so essential to life, without freedom we have nothing. A man could have a beautiful wife/harem, a six figure job, and perfect health yet if he is living by the dictates of someone else he will still be miserable. A man needs his freedom like a fish needs water. Without freedom his masculinity will be stifled it may be from an overbearing mother, a nagging wife, a asshole boss, or any number of reasons but only by living according to his own code and ideals can a man experience freedom and true manhood.

Freedom Is Essential

Freedom is essential to masculinity. Like oxygen to fire. Without freedom masculinity does survive for long. Prison takes many forms. Certain marriages, living with parents, dead end jobs, and any number of things. While you may not experience a physical prison many men are experiencing prisons of the soul. They heart is imprisoned and they don't truly feel, they don't truly live. They feel like an hollowed out shell with the fire inside reduced to ashes. Prisons of the soul can be just as bad and more permanent than prisons of the body.

As the soul is greater than the body and much more important.

There are certain steps men must take to get on the path to freedom. Freedom from the soul crushing world and society. A man was meant to be wild and free, to live his life with his soul unfettered. This is to keep the masculine spark alive and going strong. Without freedom the spark dries up and dies often to never be revived again as the man goes to his grave with his soul still in chains. I cannot imagine a sadder fate. Man was not created to be enslaved or docile but to be strong and free. To soar high and fast. Not to plod along the ground like a beast of burden or to slither on the dust like a snake. He is man, a little lower than the angels.

The Soul Of Man

What is the soul of a man? A complicated question and one that cannot be answered by one chapter or even one book. This I know a man requires freedom. Man was meant to lead, dominate, and fly. When he is shackled by women, work, or anything else he becomes like a caged animal. First he may fight against it but eventually he gives in and slowly the soul within him dies. However expose the ashes to freedom and they begin to take burn brightly once more. Some have been in prison so long they don't even remember what freedom was like.

I know that money while not the end goal plays an essential and fundamental part in freedom. That without you will not be able to fully expand your soul and yourself. I know that once money is covered you will have to cover your relations with women and your own masculinity. You will have to cover how to handle yourself in this violent world. You will have to harness your mind and bring it to work for you. To steer yourself out of your prison and into the light of freedom. You are the only one who can free yourself, you are a man no one is going to do it for you. There bill for manhood is high but worth every penny and it is a journey that never truly ends. But it runs on freedom.

Summary

Protect your freedom as your life. If you don't yet have freedom because of money or another situation work day and night to change that situation. Once money is taken care of you can expand and truly start to live. You won't constantly be preoccupied with things but be able to live in the moment. Seek freedom. Seek it like you would air if about to drown.

Freedom will revitalize you and relight the fires in your soul. The furnace that you manhood runs on. A physical prison can be fought against and you manhood retained however a soul or mental prison can destroy your manhood in a way a physical prison could never do.

This doesn't mean to never get married, or never work a office job, or anything like that. Simply that when those things encroach on your freedom they become bad. Put them in their respective places. A man values his freedom as his life, if not more than his life. As a life without freedom is not worth much. Different people may be stuck in different prisons. Most will be money, however others may vary. That is why a man must conquer all facets of his life to truly live. Guard your freedom and embrace your masculinity. You'll never regret it.

Never Tolerate Disrespect

Respect is everything. If there was one thing that I could drill into the head of men everywhere it would be to never tolerate disrespect from anyone, at any time, and at any place. There is never an excuse for disrespect. Disrespect is never something that can ignored or brushed off, it must always be addressed. I'm not saying that every time someone looks at you sideways you behead them and put their head on a pike. Simply that disrespect must be addressed. It cannot be ignored or swept under the rug, it has to be addressed.

It may be a passing remark, it may not be respecting your time, it may be trying to make you a fool in front of others. The form that the disrespect takes does not matter, it cannot be allowed to stand. If you do allow it then you will declare open season on yourself and will deserve all that you get. You can have no tolerance from disrespect. Not from your boss, not from other men, and sure as hell not from women. You are a man and must conduct yourself as such in this world, meaning never tolerating disrespect.

From Men

Knowing how to knock a guy's teeth out is always helps with not tolerating disrespect from men. Now the most common disrespect from men is going to be other men trying your mettle. Do not back down, never back down. Backing show shows weakness and you will be destroyed for it. Not saying to escalate simply address what has been said. If you let it go you declare yourself prey and will be treated as such. It could also be a sideways comment or a glance. Again no need to drive your fist through a guy's face because of an off word, address with your words and calibrate as needed.

Deep down you must have the will to fight or disrespect will be a never ending part of your life. There is a very wise saying that circulates around the America South (one of the few places where masculine white men still exist) that is essentially summed up as "Never start a fight but always finish one". Meaning don't be the dumb jackass that goes looking for a fight (great way to get yourself killed) but never back down from disrespect either. Predators are looking for an easy mark. You must not only not be an easy mark but be able to make the predator prey as well. If you would so choose.

From Women

I've seen men who would take a guy's head off for saying one word edgewise to them in the wrong tone yet sit there and let a woman berate them. Now I'm not saying you handle disrespect from women as you do men, as women and men are different. But nevertheless disrespect from women cannot be tolerated either. You must always be ready to call women out on their bullshit. Never tolerate disrespect from women. I don't care if she's the president, your mother, the hottest woman that has ever walked the earth or whatever. You do not tolerate disrespect from anyone at any time.

You must be ready and willing to put any woman in her place who shows you disrespect. Respect is everything. Without respect you have nothing. Even little breaches of disrespect must be addressed. Again not by becoming a raging maniac but by being cool, calm, and confident and pointing out the disrespect. Not politely but firmly. Firmly, calmly, and assertively. Like a man. Some women never meant it in the first place but have gone their entire lives without being told otherwise while others purposely do it. Either way it must be addressed.

Because as I've said respect is everything in any relationship.

Summary

If you tolerate disrespect you will be ripped apart. By men, by women, by everyone. A male who tolerates disrespect signals to others that he has no respect for himself and is going to be blood in the water for most. You must have respect for yourself. To make your way in this world you must take care of yourself first and foremost. You must have self-respect. Set boundaries and do not waver from them. Stick to your guiding principles and never compromise for anyone or anything.

This starts with never tolerating disrespect. Do whatever you must to address the disrespect. Do this enough and disrespect will occur less and less as all will see that you have respect for yourself and are not to be trifled with. The world in constantly testing for weakness. All will go after a weak man. Like herd animals who go after weak lions, that is because a lion is supposed to be bold, strong, and king of the jungle. And when one lets itself slide it will be destroyed by those who once feared and respected it. Being a man is no different, you must fully be the lion or perish.

Honor Your Name

We all come from somewhere. We all have a bloodline that runs through us. And we all bear a name that was shared by our male ancestors. That name means something. That name has always meant something. I guarantee your name has been fought and killed for before. There was a time when one sought to bring honor to their name. They'd fight and even kill before bringing dishonor or shame to their family name. That time is long gone. Now a man would trade his name, pride, and honor to be accepted to go along with what that latest sheeple fad is. To be accepted by a society that hates his guts.

Nothing is more disgusting and these males deserve what they get. They will have no peace in this world or the next. Your name is your blood and your blood is your everything. When you die you'll want to walk before your creator with your head held high. With your ancestors proud to share in your blood and name. There is power in a name. Utter certain names in certain places and immediately something comes to mind. Your name leaves a legacy based on how you conduct yourself.

Honor

We are told to debase ourselves for whatever society wants. That we should give up our ancestral pride and our pride in our manhood. That we should bow to false gods and serve them dutifully. Today's male focus only on being accepted rather being respected. A costly and often deadly mistake. Respect is everything. Is is more important than being accepted or being liked. The desire to be liked and accepted is the desire of a woman or child, not of a man. A man follows him own path even if it goes against the entire world around him. He cares little for he is a man.

Every deed you do whether for better of for worse gets associated with your name. You shy away from a fight and cowardice will always be associated with your name. This reflects on your father, brother, and ancestors shamefully. Likewise you make a stand you bring honor to yourself and them all. Conduct yourself accordingly. Be a role model for your sons, brothers, and all.

When I say be a role model I don't mean a role model according to society. A role model to society is a weak slave who will beg and lick the boots of those in charge. No, I mean a role model as a man. Someone who is unapologetic for who he is, is willing to fight when needed, and shows no weakness. A tall order to fill...but so what? No one said being a man was easy. Fuck easy. Do what's right, not according to society but according to your own personal code of honor. Live according to your own standards. That you never compromise for anyone or anything.

Make Them Proud

This is what man has done for centuries until the cancer of society corrupted men turning them into what we see around us today. The most powerful of creatures turned into docile weak fodder. These fodder are praised for being fodder when they should be mocked and show the error of their ways. No man should let another man get away with being weak, not if he cares about that future of that man and his offspring. Live your life so that you bring honor to your ancestors. Unfortunately in our society many are divorced from their blood and their heritage.

Know your heritage. Whatever it may be. Understand the history of your people. I don't care what your color or creed is, know your damn history. Not the history of others but your own. Know where your family name came from. I know that my blood comes from deep in the hills of Kentucky as my family line has been there since the 1700's and before that Ireland and Germany. Know who you are.

Knowing who you are helps in setting the course for your life. Sure some people get caught up in their heritage without doing anything themselves, don't be one of those people. Know where you came from, get inner strength for that. But do not think the accomplishments of your ancestors are yours, never ride the coattails of others no matter who they may be. You must forge your own life and leave your own legacy.

Summary

Bring honor to your name. When your grandchildren hear stories about you and the type of man you were they should be filled with wonder and awe. Do it for your sons and grandsons so that they have something to strive after to help them in their own development. Leave a legacy worth leaving and make your ancestors proud. Respect your blood and respect yourself. Do not let others bring you dishonor and never bow to others.

We will be judged for our conduct. When we live in dishonorable ways there are consequences in both this world and the next. Keep the sacred fire of your ancestors burning strong and brightly. Learn your own heritage so you don't become some fool trying to adopt the heritage of others. You were created who you are for a reason. Don't listen to the lies society spews about your heritage either. Remember society is the enemy to man, treat it as such.

Masculine Power

The duel forces of feminism and the MRA type movements have convinced men that they are powerless helpless victims against overwhelming forces. This is done to essentially neuter men, one does it with no bones about hurting men and the other does it through the guise of "helping" men. Telling someone they are powerless and weak and that's the way it is does in no way help men.

Men are more powerful than they could ever imagine. We are more powerful than we could ever imagine. We are not weak as society and others would have us believe.

Other than God himself man is the most powerful force that there is. It is man who created civilization and all great works. It is man who has shaped the earth around him who has harnessed the forces of nature to do his will and improve his life. This power resides in both you and me as well. The same power the resided in the heroes of old resides in us.

The Power Of Creation

Man has the power of creation. To create new life, to create great works, to create and build things. Man has the power to mold his world to how he sees fit. When you look back through history all civilizations, inventions, and further developments have been made by men. Men have shaped the course of the earth. When you look around you all that was built was built by the hands of man. The ideas you think were crafted by the minds of men. The very earth around you was shaped by men.

Single men have changed the course of history for better or for worse. Whether Hitler, Genghis Khan, or Napoleon when one man harnesses his innate power he can nearly conquer the world. It doesn't matter the society he is in or the so called limits that are placed upon him. If a man harnesses his power he can rise above it all. This isn't easy it is the innate power of man.

The Power Of Destruction

Man has the power of destruction. He can raze cities and destroy nations if he sets his mind to it. This power can be used for gain or for ill. It can be used to destroy things that are evil or it can be used to squash out what is good. But it is a power than man yields. A man can create life and build nations but he can also take life and destroy nations. Most foolishly think that this power is not good but it is, it is needed. You must know how to fight.

A man must cultivate the power to destroy those who would do him harm, no matter who they may be. We live in a fierce and unforgiving world. One where if a man doesn't cultivate this power to destroy everything he cares about and loves (even if it is only himself) can and will be taken from him and destroyed by men who did cultivate this power. Men have this capacity for fighting and destruction that must be developed. This masculine power.

Over Others

Man is the dominant force. Whatever situation he goes into he is dominant. Whether it is with woman, children, or beast man is seen as the head when he is functioning properly. Man is dominant and has power over creation. A man knows he is dominant and exercises this power. This power like all others can be used for a variety of purposes but it is a power. When a man wants to be he is seen as the authority.

An example of this is when a strong dominant man walks into a room of career women, they automatically defer to him even if they rank above him in the hierarchy. I have seen this myself women who are far above me as far as business is concerned yet defer to me because of my innate power as a man. When a man truly embraces his masculine power the world opens up before him.

Masculine Power

If you are a man you are more powerful than you can imagine. You must embrace your masculine power and fulfill your role as a man in this world. That is the only way to live a life worth living and fixing any wrongs you wish to fix. Society is created and molded by men which is why those in power fear men so, men are the only thing that can throw a wrench into the matrix. Men are the only hope that this world has. Man was created to be a little lower than the angels and the crown jewel of creation.

He has believed lies that tells him he is below women or that he is powerless when the opposite is true. Man is the head of creation. Created to rule, to create, and to destroy when needed. What has been set in stone since the beginning of time cannot be torn apart from a gang of elites of the past one hundred years. It is masculine power and masculine power alone that can bring order, balance, and healing to the world. When you were born a male you were given one of the highest honors.

Do not waste that honor.

The Foundation Of Masculinity

From where does masculinity spring? From where does it draw its power? What is the source or foundation of masculinity? These are deep questions and ones that I aim to answer in this chapter. Masculinity is something deep, primal, and powerful. It is something that one can feel in their bones, deep within their soul. It is something that can both be cultivated or destroyed. It can be built up and it can be torn down. But how? What is the underlying factor that we are looking for? What is the foundation that masculinity can be built on? The foundation that gives it it's power.

Masculinity has its foundation in freedom. When I say freedom I don't mean the Western kind meaning "rights" or where man can do as he pleases. I don't mean freedom as in freedom to be a degenerate or such nonsense as humans rights. Not that I am against human rights simply that they are a myth, society is based on force nothing more and nothing less. But that is a discussion for another time. No what I mean by freedom is the man's ability to do as he pleases when he pleases. A man kept under lock and key will always fight back or he will risk losing his soul and his masculinity in the process.

The Foundation Of Freedom

Most of us are slaves. Slaves to money, women, government, or stronger men. It is only through developing money acquiring skills, learning to be an attractive man, and learning to fight that we can truly achieve freedom and therefore a solid foundation for our masculinity and life to be based on. Through learning how to be an attractive man, money skills, and fighting skills one can truly achieve freedom. This freedom is the environment in which masculinity flourishes.

Slavery is antithetical to masculinity, masculinity must have freedom like a human must have air.

A masculine man would rather die than serve as a slave. He would rather be broken into tiny pieces than give up the most valuable thing in his possession, his freedom. He would give his life, but his freedom is never up for grabs. It is this freedom that allows one to fully and completely become a man. It is this freedom that allows one to truly experience all that we were meant to experience and become the men we were created to be. The lords of creation. This foundation of freedom is how one becomes a man. Money of which plays a key part in this freedom. Man was meant to be wild, unhinged, and untamed. An outlaw on which the basis is freedom.

Freedom The Goal

Without freedom we have nothing. Without freedom our masculinity will wilt and die. You need to have your own home, your own life, and your own way of living to be a man. You must follow your own path and be free from restraints that would be put on you to stifle your freedom and therefore your masculinity. A man cannot live in chains. If you do not have freedom this must be your number one goal. To achieve freedom. This starts with having a job that gives you freedom.

The best way to do this is to learn sales. Sales will provide you with the money that you need more so than any other skill. Better to learn sales than to learn neurology or some other complicated high paying field. I'd rather be a salesman who knew what he was doing than a doctor who spent a good chunk of his life in medical school (in slavery, unless he loved his work). I would make just as much if no more yet for a fraction of the effort. This isn't to say sales doesn't require effort just that the payoff is much higher than anything else.

After money you must conquer fighting and women. Put in other terms you must learn to assert your dominance over men and women. Men through fighting and women through attraction. You must be a dominant man in all facets of your life. This is protection against your freedom. A weak man will not remain free for long both other men and certain women will see to that. Weakness has no place in a man's life.

Freedom

A man must live free of the control of others. He must live on his own terms by following his own path. We were all put here to do a certain mission before we leave, anything that gets in the way of that is not for our benefit. As men we must avoid all things that would stifle our freedom while also doing all that we can to maximize our freedom. However you must also keep in mind freedom for the simple sake of freedom is not the end goal. Rather freedom is the foundation upon which to build your masculinity and then your life. Freedom isn't an excuse to piddle around doing nothing with your life and time.

Remember without freedom we have nothing. Take the steps needed to achieve a life of freedom so that you can develop your masculinity to new heights. Freedom is the foundation on which the good life, happiness, and your masculinity is built. Cherish it for what it is. And if you do not have it, then achieving it should be your number one goal.

3 Things Real Men Never Do

Males as a whole has fallen greatly in the past forty years. I'm sure you've seen the picture Men Then, Men Now which encapsulates what I'm talking about perfectly. Feminism combined with a myriad of other social forces, combined with men giving up and giving in has created a vortex of destruction and an unhealthy society to say the least. However giving in and hiding away do not solve anything. It never has and it never will. For things to get better men must take the fight to the enemy. And this starts by reclaiming your masculinity and reclaiming your freedom.

Here I am going to highlight three habits or traits that no strong man ever does. Yet I see these rampant in our society. Cut these traits out of your life and you'll stand head and shoulders above the poor excuse that passes for a "man" in our society. Other men will respect you, women will want you, and children will follow your lead. You will have taken another step towards fulfilling the greatest goal that there is. To be a man fully and completely, the bedrock upon which society and everything good rests.

The First Thing Real Men Never Do – Whine Or Complain

I've talked about never whining or complaining before but it bears repeating. I see many males who seem to make a sport of this. Always griping and complaining about this or that but not doing anything about it. They whine about the weather, about politics, about what's going on, about their wives. Yet do absolutely nothing about it. It's as if they just want to express and share the emotion like a woman instead of solving the problem like a man. I'm not saying men can't express emotions of course rather that men do more than that and actually work to solve a problem.

Whining doesn't do shit for you other than make you look weak. Nothing wrong with sharing but there is a difference between whining and sharing you distaste/dislike for something. Bitching has no place in a man's life. When a man is presented with a problem he gets up and he solves it. He knows complaining about it is weak and does nothing to solve the issue in the first place. If you've found your whining about something repeatedly either do something about it or shut up about it.

The Second Thing Real Men Never Do – Make Excuses

I see this all the time. Males apologizing for just about everything…even existing. I see this a lot when males interact with women. Especially when displaying interest in them. For example a male may ask a woman on a date but then immediately make some excuse for having any desire for her. Males feel they must make excuses for who they are. A real man does not make an excuse for anything that he does…he simply does it. He knows what he feels and takes action on that. If other people don't like too bad, that's their problem not his.

Doesn't mean he's a brute rather that he does his own thing. If he likes a woman he goes and tells her showing his desire openly and without excuse…just how women want. Or if they hold a unpopular political view they don't make an excuse for it they simply state their views and if someone disagrees who cares, not his problem. He doesn't need to make an excuse for anything that he does because he is confident in himself and his beliefs. He doesn't need others to validate them.

The Third Thing Real Men Never Do – Be Indecisive

A key trait of masculinity is being decisive. Making decisions and then following through on them. Like the great general Patton once said "A good plan violently executed now is better than a perfect plan executed next week". Men take charge and then they take action. They don't swing back and forth. They make up their minds and then go forward carrying out their plans. A man will pick where to go to dinner and then go. Set up a business plan and then execute. Decide he wants to bang a girl and then go after her and so on and so forth.

This isn't to say that a man never reconsiders his plans rather that he is decisive. He makes up his mind and follows through and later if he feels some adjustment is needed he does so. But he is a man of action first and foremost, the only kind there is. He doesn't sit around and wait for others to make decisions for him, he takes the responsibility and pushes things forward himself. He takes responsibility for his life and takes action to bring about what he wants. He gets shit done, put succinctly.

Summary

If you see yourself exhibiting the traits listed above now is the time to get rid of them. The first step is awareness and then taking action whenever they come up. Like stopping negative thought patterns.

The first step is to be aware there is such a thing as negative thought patterns and then to recognize them when they come up and put a stop to them. You can also actively practicing the opposite of those traits. Allowing yourself three seconds to make decisions for being indecisive and so forth.

It doesn't take much to stand out in today's world. It takes so little to be part of the elite. To stand far above the maddening crowd and to be a man in a world of boys. The be a lion among sheep. Get your habits right and everything else follows.

The Destructive Power Of Numbness

Lately I have been thinking more and more about something that has affected my life as well as the life of essentially all men at one point or another. And that is numbness. Emotional numbness in particular but numbness overall. Numbness to life. Many males numb themselves as a coping mechanism. Some do it through porn, others through booze, and yet others through sports or something else. They feel powerless and weak. But instead of rising to meet their problems they sink further and further into their numbing agents until they feel nothing at all.

To be numb is to not feel and to not feel is to not be alive. I've written about emotions before and why they are important. For one they spur men on to action. Emotions are needed to be fully and completely alive. The only thing wrong with emotions and when males let the weak ones control them otherwise emotions are essential to life and masculinity. We were not created to be tin men walking around like automatons devoid of life and spirit. Men without hearts, men without chests, men without balls.

Why We Numb Ourselves

Many males are not comfortable with their emotions. They repress them or hide them. Which isn't healthy and has consequences. The reasons we numb ourselves are many. The primary one being a coping mechanism. For example I know males who watch porn on a consistent basis yet have game and relatively good sex lives. Sometimes they say they do it even when they have no desire too. While obviously addiction and other brain chemicals are playing a huge role ultimately it comes down to being numb.

They have things in their lives that they don't want to deal with or feel like they can't deal with and therefore numb themselves with porn. Like I said earlier others do it through booze and yet others through sports and others through different means. Some do it through all of the above and more. Instead of fighting whatever is causing the problem in the first place males retreat into numbness. Because when you are numb you can't feel pain…but then again neither can you fight.

Overcoming The Numbness

Apathy can be a dangerous thing when it forced. A male if he wants can retreat from all that he hold dear. His family, his friends, even and most detrimental he can become numb from himself. From his own emotions, thoughts, and feelings until he becomes a modern zombie walking around. This is also pushed by society who wishes to have all men become listless zombies that won't fight and are easy to control. Remember it is men who change society and who can defeat the enemy

Women and children are easy to control. As long as they have no strong men to guide them. Numbness is weakness. It weakens men until they won't strike back and won't fight. Until they become patsies that can be walked on because they have lost all feelings. They have no heart and no balls. That is what numbness does. A man who feels with his heart and soul is a fearsome force feared by those who stand against him and revered by those he stands for. Numbness is like defanging a lion or neutering a wolf. But it can be overcome.

Steps To Reconnect

First and foremost you must reconnect with yourself. You must reconnect with your heart and soul. You must reconnect to the seat of your power. First off you must cut out whatever it is that is your main numbing agent. If it's booze cut it out. If it's porn cut it out. If it's sports reduce it to social functions (the same could be said with booze, but no exceptions are to be made with porn). Begin journaling what you feel.

Upon waking write down what is on your heart. It is there for a reason. Connect with that and you will connect with yourself. You will begin reconnecting with your masculine power. You will begin to feel again. Evil will make you sick as will weakness. You will begin holding yourself to a standard. You will begin to get your fight back. You will begin to get your manhood back. Those in control don't want this because men are the only ones who can change the path this world is on.

The Roaring Lion

When the lion roars the wolves scatter. Remember you are powerful. The evils of the world have gone unopposed for too long. The dragons and giants run through the land because men have disappeared from it. When the heroes return the monsters run. You were given a heart and soul for a reason and to divorce yourself from the two was not the reason. Take the fight to them.

If all become numb there will never again be a David, a Solomon, a Achilles, a Ulysses, a Arthur, a Martel, a Lionheart, a Leonidas, a Washington, a Jackson, or a Patton. All will become sheep and led to the slaughter. It is men and men alone that can prevent this. Numb men do not fight they lie down. Fight against this reconnect with yourself and rekindle the fire that lies within.

How To Talk Like A Man

What does it mean to talk like a man? Does it mean to say "bro" a lot as well as curse as much as possible? No, not at all. Does it mean to always use polite language and be respectful of women? Fuck no. I bring up two examples because they are ones I've heard before and made me write this chapter. In case you haven't noticed males today aren't the best at communicating with one another (not that women are much better). Once schools taught rhetoric but it was done away with (probably to make room for gender-queer studies).

If you watch a show like Mad Men you'll notice that the characters have a way of talking and addressing one another that we do not nowadays. Not that the show is a perfect example but I think you'll understand what I'm getting at. Point is males need to be taught how to talk like a man instead of a little boy. There is a certain way that a man talks that distinguishes himself from the beta hordes. Here is what it is.

Men Project When They Talk

What I mean by this is when a man speaks he makes sure he is heard. He uses adequate volume. This does not mean he goes around yelling and shouting but rather he uses enough force to make sure he is heard. He uses the right amount of volume. He doesn't whisper like so many males do nowadays. He isn't afraid to be heard and this can be heard from the way he talks. Again not yelling but projecting.

No one should ever have to ask "What did you say?". Obviously this requires calibration in a loud environment such as a football game it may require yelling while in a dinner it may just require talking with some force behind it. When you project you are going to speaking from your "chest" voice and not your "nose" voice. Your chest voice has much more power and is deeper sounding and is how men are supposed to talk.

Men Enunciate When They Talk

How many people do you know who mumble when they talk. They say something and you're lef scrambling to figure out just what the hell it is that they said. Cut this shit out. When you speak enunciate every word and syllable. Make it clear what you say and what you mean. Don't mumble or put words together give every word the space that it needs. You don't have to sound like a phonetics track but make sure that every syllable is said completely and fully.

Mumbling is when you put your words together and don't give them the space that they need. Respect every word that comes out of your mouth. If you're taking the time to say it, then it is worth listening too. People who mumble also come across as being scared that people will hear what they are saying or that they are used to being ignored so don't put the time and effort into speaking correctly. Neither of which is very masculine. Enunciate every word.

Men Talk Slowly

Men take time with what they have to say. They aren't rushed nor are they nervous. The let words linger and don't mind if there is gaps in what they are saying. They assume others will hang on their every word and because of this assumption they generally do. Take time with your words and sentences. Don't be afraid to put pauses and breaks in there if needed. You've probably heard males who speak as if if they don't get everything out with one breath they'll explode.

This is not confident behavior and therefore not masculine. It makes you sound weak and afraid. Weak males are always worried about being interrupted so they hurry their words. While men speak slowly because they know they will be heard not to mention this improves comprehension of what you say. Point is talk slowly and take your time. The vast majority of people talk way too fast. Especially when they're in front of a crowd. Slow down your speech.

Summary

So there you have it, three simple easy to follow tips to sound more masculine as well as be a better speaker. I think rhetoric is a very important skill and one that all men need to master at one point or another. For some reason communication gets billed as something for women why this is I have no idea especially since all the greatest communicators and networkers throughout history have always been men. Point is you must learn to communicate both in the written word and in face to face interactions.

3 Areas You Must Be Proficient In To Call Yourself A Man

Usually whenever I see a headline that has to do with being a man I know I'm going to puke, especially with the mainstream media. However this is different. This chapter isn't about what some liberal yuppie boy thinks is going to sound good to his female boss, this is about actual manhood. Manhood is about many different things, one of the key things being the development of skills and knowledge in certain key areas. The three areas that are listed here are by no means an exhaustive list but they do provide a solid foundation upon which to expand.

Going from boy to man is not something that happens automatically like when a girl becomes a woman. Your balls dropping doesn't mean you have become a man. You may have gone from boy to male but not from boy to man. That requires work and the acquirement of certain skills. Much of life really comes down to acquiring and stacking skills. These three skills are the most essential to learn to live a life filled with freedom and to be fully a man.

The First Skill – Business

By business I mean pretty much anything and everything related to the skill of acquiring money. This could include things like learning a trade, copywriting, marketing, and sales to things like having an entrepreneurial mindset. Point is you have to learn to support yourself. You can't be fully a man and be reliant on mommy and daddy, the government, or even a corporate job where your boss could can you at any moment (and probably will, especially if you don't belong to a protected class). You must be independent and be able to take care of yourself.

You cannot rely on others to employ you or to keep you afloat. That "secure" job you have now working for someone you respect could do a complete 180 when next month a new company buys it, fires your boss, and proceeds to make your life a living hell before firing you for kicks at the end. Learn business skills or get screwed, learn how to handle yourself or get used to getting trampled on by others. This is the harsh reality of the world. Work for someone else and you'll always be a slave. You must know how to go out and acquire money for yourself.

The Second Skill – Seduction

In addition to knowing how to go out and get money you must also know how to go out and get women. Having an understanding of women is just as important as having an understanding of money. A boy can't just hope to end up with the right girl and just hope that his marriage will last. He must take deliberate actions to have the relationship with women that he wants. Whether that's a rotating harem or a family it doesn't matter. Neither will be successful without and understanding of women and how to seduce them.

You must know how to be irresistible to women. Look every man wants a woman. Even men who hate women still have sexual feelings for them just like feminists still have sexual desires for men, especially masculine men. Because despite their hate or programming (whether feminist or MRA) they still have their same biology. You can't go through life a virgin and be fulfilled. The biological urge is too strong. Reproduction is from a biological standpoint our highest calling and one we must be able to fulfill (even if we don't choose to do so).

The Third Skill – Survival

There was a time when weak males were naturally culled by nature leaving only the strong. While we don't live in a world where we have to worry about being a tiger's lunch we still need to be able to defend ourselves. Even if you never have to call on your survival skills you still need to have them. Sort of like insurance you may never need it but when you do need, you need it really bad. You may never have to throw a punch or draw on someone but the second you do, you'd better be prepared.

Just like in seduction we have the sexual pyramid in survival there are categories of males as well. Criminals know this. They prey on those that are unsuspecting and show weakness, just like bullies. I'm not saying you have to become a Navy SEAL or anything simply know how to handle yourself in a dangerous situation. Learn how to fight. You may never need it that doesn't mean it is not an essential skill to learn.

Summary

Becoming proficient in these three skills will put you ahead of the pack and ensure that you have a high quality of life that cannot be taken away from you. You will be able to withstand whatever the world throws at you. You will laugh at recessions, shit tests, and criminals because you know how to handle each and every one. Nothing will shake you, you will be a man. Standing firm in the world while everything collapses and changes around you. You will be the oak in the storm, the mountain that never changes.

Don't be the man who builds his house upon the sand (what the mainstream says you need to learn) but instead build your house upon the rock (what reality says you need to learn) and when the rains come you will not be fazed. And always remember be a man and everything else falls into place. If you have sons or younger male relatives I would strongly encourage you either share this chapter (or even this book) with them or at least convey to them the meaning. They will thank you down the line, as will I.

The Right Order To Learn These Skills For Maximum Effect

All the skills talked about in the previous chapter have value and of course they're all important but there is a way to get the most from them in the least amount of time possible. And as time is our most valuable resource it is wise to make the best use of it. I should also not that there are some fundamentals that need to be covered before one throws himself in mastering (or becoming proficient in the skills).

Also a word about mastery. Don't master one skill before moving onto the next. Simply become proficient in each in the order they are listed here and then after you are proficient in all master them all. Otherwise you'd take too long to get the maximum advantage from each because you'd be focused on mastering a skill. For example you don't have to be worth one hundred million dollars before you can focus on getting your sex life where you want it to be with the women you want it to be with likewise you'd don't have to be able to go ten rounds with Tyson before learning how to make money, etc. You get the point.

The Foundation

But before we get to the skills there is something you need to understand first for the skills to have a solid foundation to rest on. And that thing is mindset. You can have all the skills in the world but if you have a faulty, negative, victim mindset none of it will matter. You have to learn to believe in yourself and use your mind for you, not against you. Perhaps this sounds cheesy or a bit basic. Nevertheless it is the foundation upon which all else is built. If you have the wrong mindset you'll fail. You can't stand in your own way.

This is best summed up in the quote by the great industrialist Henry Ford "Whether you think you can or think you can't…you're right". Now mindset alone is not enough to take you to the life you want but it is the foundation upon which all else is built. This is why you have one person who thinks having a good mindset is all they need yet they're poor broke losers while another says mindset is key and is a rich successful winner. Mindset is the key but it is not the end all be all. Get your mind right before all else. You can't fight a battle against yourself you will lose. Understand the importance of mindset and get your mind on your own side.

The Basics

Now that you understand how your mind works and understand the importance of it we can begin with the skills. However we are not going to specialize just yet. First thing we need to do is have a rudimentary knowledge of each of the three skills. Combat, women, and money. Not a in depth or even proficient knowledge but just enough to put us above the level of the average person. This would require a few books to understand and then practice. Here is what I recommended pick up How To Get

Girls: The Definitive Guide That'll put you ahead of 90% of people and you'll have no problem getting laid with some decent girls. It'll also prevent you from doing something stupid like getting married to the wrong chick or wasting your time being a woman's emotional tampon and so on and so forth.

I would also recommend you pick up Championship Fighting by Jack Dempsey and do the routine outlined in it. You'll be a better fighter than 90% of people out there after a few months of dedicated training. Again we're not mastering the skills here (or even becoming proficient) just getting a taste for each. Like I said if you mastered money buy got married to a woman who was going to divorce raped you because you never learned the basics about women you'd be screwed. Which is why a basic knowledge of all is essential become becoming proficient at each. Also I'd recommend The Millionaire Fastlane and Bachelor Pad Economics to get you started on the path the economic understanding as well as how the corporate world will grind you down and spit you out. As well as the stupidity of going to college.

Money Comes First

Money is the first skill that you need to become proficient in. You understand everything there is to know about women and be able to get them to hop in bed with you after five minutes as well as being able to punch out way above your weight class and the best gunslinger since Jesse James yet if you're still living with your parents you're not going to feel like a man. I want to make something clear to you and have it linked in your mind. Money equals freedom. Let me repeat that money equals freedom. Now you may say "Sledge man I know guys who make bank but spend 80 hours a week to get it" or something to that extent.

Those men are foolish as they are trading their freedom for money. They mistake money for the end goal when freedom is the end goal. Yet nevertheless money is freedom. Without money you can never achieve freedom but if you make money the end goal you'll miss out on freedom as well. Sales, copywriting, and marketing. Become proficient in each as well as having a general understanding of business and how to make money in our economy. Sales is essential to this. I would start with learning all there is to learn about sales. Then get a job that is paid on commission, you'll make bank if you truly understand this. I'd also do a side hustle to start building in passive income. So combine sales knowledge with passive income. Once you're getting in around 5k a month at least 1k of which is from passive income you can start branching out into other skills.

Women Come Next

Look as a guy you're going to want to have a good sex life with beautiful women. Women play a large part in a man's life and this is the way it's supposed to be. I know others feel differently about this but this is how I see it. I want sex and as long as I'm healthy and have testosterone flowing through my veins I'll continue to want it. And I want it with the most beautiful women. Yet with no knowledge of the way women work and what they respond too I'll not be able to have a sex life with the beautiful women I want. Pretty simple right? Anyways learning all I can about attraction allows me to master this and get the sex life I want.

Porn is no substitute for real women and neither is prostitution. Maybe it's the hunter in me but I get no joy from paying for sex and would feel weak because of it. Others have other opinions but that's mine. I enjoy the dynamic of seduction and going out. I enjoy beautiful women and their company.

Women are only a pain if you don't know how to handle them and don't put them in their place. Remember women are reactive, they respond to you. I don't believe a man can live a full life without any interaction with women even if it's only sexual. Master them and you'll get the sex life you want. Once you have a couple of good looking girls who give you what you want in the rotation and know you can go out and get more anytime you want it's time to become proficient in combat.

Combat Is Third

There was a time when combat was the ultimate skill for a man to learn. When killing was a man's way of life. These times are long gone but that doesn't mean this skill no longer has any value for a man. Humans will always be humans and a man must always know how to fight. Humans at their base are animals, and animals prey upon one another. You could have all the money in the world and have beautiful women surrounding you yet if some random angry thug could put you in the dirt you have very little power. The unaware and unprepared are weeded out sooner or later. This still applies. Those who are prepared and have the skills to defend themselves survive plain and simple.

Prey gets eaten and humans are no exceptions. Soft targets get destroyed. As a man you must be able to defend yourself against threats. Whether that threat is the drunk at the bar who followed you out to your car, the punk who tried to rob you, or an extremist bent on your destruction. A man must be able to fight, kill, and survive. He must understand how to use his fists, tools, surroundings, and mind to kill other men. You may say "In our society most will never have to use these skills" but all it takes is one encounter to make it all worth it. When you walk away from a potentially deadly encounter with your life it'll all be worth it. And it's never smart to hope that you'll never run into violence. Hoping will never get you anything good and in this case may result in your death. Learn combat. Learn to use your fist and gun at a proficient level.

Then What?

After that you are free to pursue whatever skill gives you the most bang for your buck. Maybe you want to bang lots of beautiful women across the world, perhaps you want to reach Navy SEAL levels of proficiency in combat, or perhaps to want to become the next Donald Trump. No matter what I'd encourage you to constantly develop all three skills until you have them all mastered and then go even higher. Learn the skills in this order for maximum effect and best use of your time and watch your life soar to heights only dreamed about.

We Were Born To Be Wild

There are many facets that distinguish a man from a male and even more so a man from a woman. Facets such as being unapologetic, being dominant, and being a leader. There is a certain energy that surrounds a man that others can feel and sense, especially women. Much of this has to do with how much a man is fulfilling his biological function. Despite advances in civilization (for the most part) we still retain the same biology that we were created with and that our ancestors have. What makes a man a man and a woman a woman is something that never has changed and never will change.

A large part of being a man is being free. A male who is henpecked by his wife, abused by his boss, and treated like dirt by society will not feel like a man. His testosterone will take a dive as will his manhood. He will feel and weak and feeble. And because our mind creates our reality eventually he will be weak and feeble if he sticks in the same rut. Man was born to be wild. He was born to be free. However unlike in the age of our ancestors where a man was given the freedom to roam, fight, and procreate now we live in a unnatural and unhealthy society that stifles men and masculinity at every turn.

Born To Be Wild

Man was never made to follow the rules. This why a movie like *Fight Club* had and has such a large appeal to so many men. The feelings of powerlessness and being castrated by a society that could give a shi about you. Man was never meant to be a pawn, to be a cog in the machine. Man was meant to fulfill his place with his brothers in a loyal tribe. To fight against the world with his brothers by his side. Not to rot away in a cubicle and get called into HR for daring uttering some word deemed "improper" by a bunch of soulless yuppies.

My point is man wasn't meant to live as a castrated slave. Man was meant to live free or die. Not to work away making someone who hates his guys richer and more powerful day by day. However modern society is designed just to do that. However you do not have to live this way. You can take back your freedom from those that would deny it to you and claim your destiny as a man.

It's Not Easy, It's Worth It

To reclaim your freedom is no easy task but it is worth it. It is as the cadets of West Point would say "the harder right over the easier wrong". It takes skills to reclaim your freedom, skills that society not only will not teach you but will tell you it is wrong to learn. Skills such as game, entrepreneurship, and how to fight. Skills that make you less and less dependent on society and more and more independent. Society does not want you to be wild and free. Wild and free men make for poor slaves.

There are steps to take on your path to freedom that must be taken as soon as possible. This is not something you can wait for. There is no better time than now. Your chains aren't going to get any lighter son. In all likelihood you friends, family, and certainly any woman in your life will be against this (at least at first). Unplugging from the matrix is something they see as dangerous and risky. Better to just keep your head ducked and keep plugging away. But you know better. You know they don't want you to unplug from the matrix because of the power and freedom it gives to you so they tell you it's dangerous.

Freedom Over The Illusion Of Safety

Safety is an illusion. Even if you toe the line and follow all the rules like a good slave doesn't mean you'll end up alright. Ask the men who loyally worked for a company for thirty plus years only to be canned because they need to diversify the staff more. Or the man who did everything his wife asked and said for him to do only to walk in on her banging some asshole. Or the man who always voted leftist truly believed the diversity is strength and then got his ass beat by some thugs.

You have to rely on yourself you are the only person that you can rely on. Understanding this is the beginning of unplugging from the matrix and taking back the very foundation of your manhood. Safety is an illusion, freedom is not. Take the harsh truth over pleasant lies because it is only the harsh truth that can set you free. At first it'll suck but you must embrace the such man up and get through it. There is no room in this life for whining or complaining, not for winners anyways. Not for men.

Summary

Man is not a domestic animal but rather a wild one that has been domesticated by an unnatural and unhealthy society. This isn't to say civilization in and of itself is unhealthy simply the way modern civilization is run. You can free yourself from the chain and once more howl at the moon and run through the glades. Reclaiming your freedom is hard but it is worth every moment. Nothing on this earth can replace the feeling of knowing you answer to no one but yourself and that you truly have freedom.

We Are All Called To Be Leaders

As a man to get the most out of life there are some things that are non-negotiable and that if we lived in a healthy society we would have been taught since birth. Things like how to make money, the reality of women, and the importance of combat skills. As well as how the mind affects all that we do and how freedom cannot be achieved unless we master ourselves and the preceding skills. I've written before about why the man must lead when he interacts with a woman but the truth is it goes much deeper than that.

A man must lead in all that he does. Every man must be a leader of himself and the world around him. Remember men are the active forces of creation. If a man wants something done then he must go out and do it himself making it essential for men to learn certain skills. If a man sits back and waits for others he'll end up dead, he needs to take things on himself and sarge forward.

Leadership

Like being unapologetic and dominant being a leader is an essential part of manhood. A man must lead in all that he does. He must lead when seducing a woman, he must lead when he has a family, he must lead in business, he must lead with other men, he must lead in everything. As a man you must take everything upon yourself and then refine yourself to the point where you can deal with it all. The earlier you start taking responsibility for where you are the earlier you'll have a great life.

I've talked before about taking charge of your own life and this is essentially what leadership is. Taking responsibility which requires strength. It's much easier to blame others, circumstances, or to just gaze at your navel hoping for the best. However it is not masculine and it will do you no favors. Men are the leaders, women, children, and males are the followers.

Everyone Is Looking To You

Our society is falling apart because men have let it. This may sound harsh but it is the truth. Something like feminism could be easily resolved if the males of Western society weren't too weak to stand against it. Feminism is a shit test that has been failed on a massive scale. However men who ignore the delusions of feminism are rewarded with submissive women and massive amounts of attraction from all women.

Women are not leaders, can never be leaders, and perhaps most surprising don't want to be leaders. They weren't created for it and fail horribly when the leadership position is given to them. A man who hands the guidance of his family over to his wife only has himself to blame when his family falls apart. A woman will never respect a man who gives the reins over to her. You are the captain of your life.

Ownership

There is no room for whining or complaining in a man's life. If something goes wrong it is because he has failed at some level. At first this might sound extreme or neurotic but on closer inspection it is actually the thing that will lead to the most growth and development. You are shoving yourself into the deepest level of the fire so that you will come out the hardest of steel. As a man we either rise as heroes or fall to the wayside as weak fodder fit for the vultures. This isn't fair, but life has never and will never be about what is fair.

Once you embrace this harsh reality you will be able to gain strength from it. This doesn't mean we cannot support each other as brothers or that the few good women left won't support you. It simply means that you shouldn't count on it. Go into the fight as if it'll just be you against the world because it most often will be. Then when others are there to help you it will be even easier. However it cannot be counted upon. A man must be independent and free.

Summary

The more responsibility you take for where you are in life the more power you will gain. A man must lead in all that he does, and I do mean all. You must be hard on yourself because the world will crush any male who exhibits weakness. Weakness in a male is seen as something to exploit unlike weakness in a woman or child. Purge yourself of weakness (though not feeling) and become the man that you were created to be. It is a blessing to be a man, embrace it and go forth and conquer.

How To Save Western Civilization & The World

A hefty topic for a single chapter but one that I believe can be adequately addressed in a mere one thousand words, give or take a few. It's no secret that our world is crumbling around us. The elites have designed to usurp the natural order and replace it with their own. They have turned race against race, woman against man, child against parent, and so on and so forth. This has all been engineered and done on purpose. While more and more are becoming aware of this the question then changes too what is to be done about it?

What can simple men do against those who hold the money and the power? It seems like a hopeless fight. But that is not so. The powerful have been defeated, unrighteous kings thrown out, and healthy society reclaimed and held for a time. But there are some things that are required for such a thing to take place. The natural thing is to focus on the outside. But this is wrong.

Focusing On Others

Many believe if just person X were gone everything would be better without realizing that the ones you see out in the lime light are really nothing more than replaceable puppets. If they fall they will simply be replaced. Another thought it to go to the source and eliminate it but even then those who want us dead and destroyed will always come back up. Not to mention finding the enemies in their webs of lies and trickery is nearly impossible to do. For every George Soros we hear about there are ten in the shadows we know little to nothing about.

There will always be the wolves in the dark looking to take what is precious to us. Whether that is our own life and well-being or the life and well-being of our family (in addition to ourselves). Until the end we will have to fight against them and they will always be with us. That is the way of the world. This isn't to say that fighting them is wrong, it is right on every level. Simply to point striking down one enemy will not save us from having to fight again tomorrow.

What Makes A Civilization Great

What is responsible for the rise and fall of civilization? What both creates and destroys civilizations? Many would say certain forms of government, others would say women, and others would say demographics. Yet it always comes back to the same factor. And that is the men of the society. A society filled with strong men cannot be preyed on by the likes of Soros and his kind, nor could something like feminism come about because the men would stomp it out before it knew what happened, likewise no invaders would come because they would be destroyed.

The world rises and falls based on the actions of men. Strong men in particular. As the wise Edmund Burke once said "The only thing needed for the triumph of evil is for good men to nothing". Good men meaning masculine strong men, not castrated sheep as the word "good" has come to mean. With these good men society falls into line and growth happens. Unfortunately many, especially those deemed "red pill" have become cynical, they see society as unsavable, women as unredeemble, and life as nothing more than banging as many hot chicks as possible until they eventually die.

It Starts With You

This doesn't lead to a fulfilling life. Of course it's better than marrying some ho and getting divorced raped while she cuckolds you but there are so many other options out there for life. It isn't a black and white deal. But the short falls of the red pill is a topic for another time. This chapter is about saving Western civilization. And saving Western civilization all starts with you. Let me explain why. A healthy world is forged by healthy nations, healthy nations are forged by strong tribes, strong tribes are formed by strong families, and strong families are only forged and upheld by strong men.

Women and children left to their own devices would have the world in flames within a week. They cannot lead themselves. If all men were "red pill" aware meaning aware of how society, biology, and life works the world would be a much healthier place. But it all starts with making yourself strong, to be the example that others can look after. The leaders that this world so desperately needs, the heroes that bring it back from the edge. Of course this does start with knowing how to get laid, make money, and fight. Once those are covered then a man focuses on the fate of society as a whole.

Summary

Saving Western civilization starts and ends with men becoming men again. The more this happens the more the cancer that has the world in its grasp will retreat and be beaten. Those against us are not invincible and our belief that they are is their greatest strength. The natural order can be returned to, the fight can be one. Perhaps you are already too far gone and that is fine. Everyone walks their own path. But me I will stand and make myself great. And eventually lead a family in the restoration. You are free to join me and I hope you will.

It Sucks To Suck

There is no one coming to save you. Boys growing up aren't told this enough. As a man you must forge yourself into a man capable of facing this world or you will be crushed by it. There is no safety net for men. The world has no pity for a weak male. You will be crushed, spat on, and used if you don't not rise and become powerful. This might sound harsh, that's because it is. It might sound unfair, that's because it is. But most important it is the truth. A man either rises and soars like the eagle or is trodden underfoot like the worm. Men sink or swim, they don't float.

The world is not a nice or a friendly place. You experience freedom in this world there are so many things that a man must master. Just like the only countries who can have peace are those with who it is too costly to go to war with. It is the same with men. The only way for a man to have peace is to be powerful. It's important to take this gut shot earlier rather than later. The earlier it is understood the better off you will be.

It Sucks To Suck

It sucks to suck. Any male who seeks pity will only be destroyed. Males must man up or they will be ran straight over. Unlike women and children who can be weak and get a pass this option does not exist for males and it never will. A male is thrown into the wolves' den and expected to come out alive. The strong make it and the weak do not. Many males have been raised to believe that they can be like women, clueless and adrift (not that all women are like this) and come out fine.

But that is not going to happen. Governments, religions, and the world itself has no pity or remorse for a weak male and sees him as nothing more than an easy target. When the storm rages, when the wolves are at the door, there is no refuge or hiding place for a man. His only option is to stand and fight. The outcome being either victory or death. A man can only have comfort in relation to his power and strength. And even then comfort should never even be close to a man's top priority.

Master Himself

However being a man is not all doom and gloom. For when a male forged himself into a man then the tables turn. Women and children can never learn to swim only float around. A man can be trodden on or he can take flight, women and children simply plod along. However this flight only takes place when a man has mastered himself and has undergone the transformation from boy to man. It cannot and will not happen before that time.

A man must embrace and understand his innate masculinity. He must become master over women, over wealth, and over battle. To the modern neutered male this might sound old fashioned or "out there" but it is the truth. In more stable societies it probably isn't this bad but the society we live in is against men, family, and the health of society. The media, government, law system, corporations, and just about everything else will be against you. You must be strong to survive.

Put Yourself Through The Fire

Imagine how much more soldiers would be shell shocked if they never went through basic training. How much more they would be torn apart. It is only through dedicated training that they are able to keep a handle on being sent into battle (and sometimes that isn't enough). Males need to undergo training to make it in this world as well or they will be torn to little pieces when they are thrown into the wolves den. As all males eventually are. I noted above that this training will have to do with mastering oneself, as well as the realms of women, wealth, and battle.

Fathers used to train their sons to be able to make it in the world but no more. The generation before us has failed us on every single last level, we must take it into our own hands to become men. Believe it or not but for me this all began with reading. Getting exposed to a different way of thinking that eventually led me to embracing my masculinity and rising up.

Summary

No one is coming to save you. You must do it on your own and lead yourself out of the situation that you are in. You have to pull yourself out by your bootstraps or you will sink and die in the mud. At first this realization may piss you off especially when you've been indoctrinated in blue pill thinking. But reality is reality regardless of how you feel. And remember what waits for you on the other side.

The Top 10 Most Important Skills For A Man To Master

The quality of your life is for the most part dependent on the skills that you have learned and mastered. Most boys go through life never mastering any skills that are truly related to their development as men and the quality of their life. Never forget following the mainstream is a great way to end up angry and miserable. By mastering the skills below you are going to avoid a lot of the pain that the average male goes through and create a life that you'll love.

Of course there are no guarantees in life but mastering these skills is as close as you are going to get. Lately we've been talking about how to acquire skills and now that you know that it's time to address what skills are the most important to acquire. Mastering these skills are going to give you a chance at freedom, and being able to live out your dreams. Whatever they may be.

Note: These skills are in a random order and should all be learned.

Skill #1 – Combat

This isn't a skill you're typically going to find on most "skills men need" list but it is essential. At the very core of our being we get a large portion of our worth from how well we are able to handle violence and threats. A man who cannot handle a violent enemy is not a man. Plain and simple.

You must know how to fight. This includes using your body (unarmed) and weaponry (armed). You must know how to throw a punch, defend against an attacker, and a basic use of firearms. You don't have to be a sharp shooter or a boxing champ but you must be able to defend yourself adequately. You cannot be a sheep in a world of wolves. You must be a lion, the alpha predator.

Skill #2 – Basic Survival

If you were left out in the wilderness for three days would you know how to survive? If not then you need to learn this. Sheltered souls might think that skills like this are no longer needed but they could not be more wrong. Like I said at our most basic level masculinity is about surviving and fighting. When we cannot do that we can never be fully men. Know how to construct a basic shelter, how to acquire water and food, and start a fire.

Not exactly rocket science but important skills to learn. I would recommend going into the woods and trying this for small periods of time. Even if just a night. Just you, the wilds, and your survival tools. Man needs to be connected with his wild side and with his primal soul. This connection gets severed working as a cubicle drone and when in a marriage with an unfeminine Western woman. Reconnect with nature, reconnect with your soul.

Skill #3 – Masculinity

"How is masculinity a skill?" you might ask. This is frankly a bit nebulous but needs to be on here.

While I wouldn't necessarily consider masculinity a "skill" it is something that every man must come to master and grow in. A man must operate from his masculine core. With a fire in his heart. Think of it this way you can look at two men and tell which is more masculine than the other. And it has little to do with their outside features.

It is something that is much deeper, something that is on a heart and soul level. You must embrace, foster, and grow this. You must harness your masculine power. This is where everything else is going to stem from. Many of the skills are this list will feed into your masculinity but they are not replacements for it. Everything from speaking your mind to standing your ground grows your masculinity. Master this. And never forget dominance plays a huge role.

Skill #4 – Mindset

You've probably heard that "mindset is everything" this is true. A man who has a mind that is working against him is never going to get anywhere. You must master your mind because your mind is the master. A man with a good mindset can overcome any obstacle but in his way while a man who has a bad mindset will no matter how many advantages he is given. You must take control of this powerful instrument and use it to better your life.

Thoughts are things and they have a huge impact on your life. Your thoughts make up a large part of your life. Having negative thoughts results in a negative mindset having productive thoughts results in a productive mindset and so on and so forth. You must learn to use your mind to shape your destiny. The mind is incredibly powerful make sure that this power is used for your gain.

Skill #5 – Soft Skills

I'm including sales skills, networking, and being likable under this umbrella of soft skills. They all have to do with dealing with people in a positive and productive way. Humans are social animals and to get what you want out of life you are going to have to learn to deal with them and how they operate. You need to learn how to get people on your side and get what you want from them while also benefiting them.

You must know how to network not just for business purposes but because we live in a world with a million distractions and people going every which way. Even to form a tribe you are going to have to learn how to network. Bringing people into the fold is an important skill especially with how disconnected people are nowadays. Sales is getting what you want from others and is important for obvious reasons.

Skill #6 – Copywriting/Marketing

Financial independence was once a nice dream for a select few. Now it's a requirement if you want to live a life worth living. Never have corporations been more feminized, poorly run, or political making them toxic places for men. You will be a slave to some drying up angry woman, political correct

HR, and a boss who sees you as a cog that can replaced when it wears down from hard work. Get the hell out of the corporate world as soon as you can.

But in order to do this and do this successfully you will have to learn copywriting and marketing. Take a master copywriter/marketer give him any business and he can make it successful (barring some extreme examples). Your product/service really doesn't matter, but your copywriting and marketing skills matter more than you can imagine. Get started on these skills so you can realistically plan your escape to freedom.

Skill #7 – Health

None of this is going to matter if you are in poor health. You don't have to become a bodybuilder or a fitness freak (who aren't very healthy anyway) but you should be in good shape and have a reasonably healthy diet. Don't make fitness your god as many do. Fitness is no replacement for masculinity or things of that manner. But it is very important you want to grow old and in good health. But don't become obsessive over this.

Stay away from sugar and grains. Limit your intake of processed foods. Hit the gym at least three times a week. Get at least eightish hours of good sleep. Don't become obsessed about this. God knows why but of all the skills this is the one people throw their entire life into with rapidly decreasing ROI. Remember the Pareto Principles eighty percent of your results come from twenty percent of your efforts and nowhere does this hold more true than health.

Skill #8 – Attraction

Look if you are healthy and normal than woman are going to play a huge part in your life and this is a good thing. However if you fail to understand them then you will get burned. Women are either going to be one of the number one sources of pleasure and fun in your life or they are going to be the number one source of pain. All depending on if you have mastered this skill or not. You need to understand women for who they are and not what you've been told they are.

Whether it's manosphere lies that all women are lying, cheating, evil whores or the mainstream's women are perfect, can do no wrong, and holy. Women are human and created to be man's helper. When weak males let them run wild then bad things happen. Just like if we let children do whatever they want. There are different women that are good for different things.

There are women who are good for banging and nothing more and women who are good for raising children with and many others. You must master women.

Skill #9 – The Language Of Composition

The language of composition is reading, writing, and rhetoric. Put another way you must master reading (yes it's a skill), writing, and speaking. Communication is fundamental to life success. I'm not sure why people think this is optional. If our schooling system was intelligent (cue laughter) we'd have kids master this before anything else (in addition to logic) but instead they are too busy being indoctrinated.

You must take it upon yourself to master these skills. You don't have to become a combination of Shakespeare and Cicero but you need to have a basic grasp of good writing and speaking. Reading is pretty straightforward. Read a lot and you get good at it, not the mention will change your life. Learn to communicate through both the written word and the spoken word, few ever do.

Skill #10 – Logic

Long ago before schools were simply places where children were sent to be indoctrinated into the latest Communist nonsense they were a place of learning. Students coming out of school had a leg up on those who did not attend (what a concept) and a large part of this had to do with students learning basic logic. Call it critical thinking or simply "not being a dumbasss" but logic is a fundamental skill to live a successful life.

Unfortunately most textbooks on logic are bogged down by political ideology (a bit ironic) but you can still learn this skill by teaching it to yourself. What it really comes down to is putting thought into the things you do. Just taking a second to think about things. For example when doing an activity thinking "is this a productive use of my time?". Ask questions and don't swallow things hook, line, and sinker. Not hard but rarely done.

Summary

Mastering these skills will put you above the level of 99% of humans, above the level of 99% of men even. You'll officially be a one percenter. Others around you will struggle and fight every day of their lives only to get nowhere and often end up even worse than they were. This will put you into a position where you can either help others and lead them to freedom or laugh as the world burns. Your choice. The point is mastering these skills puts the power in your hands, and gives you the freedom to do what you want with your life. And after all isn't that what it's all about.

How To Gain Power In 3 Key Areas Of Your Life

Without power we are nothing. Without power we will be crushed by the world. Acquiring power is your duty to survive. A man who doesn't spend a good portion of his time in the pursuit and development of his power is always taken advantage of and killed off by the world. This is a harsh lesson that is best learned young so that a man doesn't get hit with it too late in life. If a man is to protect himself and those he loves and what he holds dear he must acquire power in these three areas of life.

You already know what the three areas are as I've talked about them before in this book. Combat, business, and relations with women. Weakness in any of these areas will get a man killed. So finding out the best way to ensure you are prepared to deal with these areas is a wise use of your time. You must declare war on any weakness you may have to make sure you can live a happy good life. Power is the only thing that can ensure this. Power ultimately is the only thing that matters. Morality means nothing without power, love means nothing without power, nothing means anything without power.

Sales Gives You Power In Business

Sales, sales, sales. This skill isn't negotiable. It isn't optional. It's required. You need to learn sales as much as you needed to learn how to read and write. Not knowing sales in the business world would be like getting dropped into a war zone without a gun. Sales is your weapon to get what you want in the business world. It's your claws, fangs, and means of defense. Those who know sales succeed and those who don't know sales die. It's a pretty black and white issue. Don't rely on good connections (but have them), skill at what you do (like that means anything in the modern corporate world), and least of all on the good will of those around you.

You have to become a great salesman for success in life. No other skill even comes close to getting what you want in business. If you feel powerless in business then you aren't a ballsy enough salesman. The weak and timid get destroyed and left for the vultures. It doesn't matter if you're not in a "sales" job because every job is a sales job. There is nothing that will make you more valuable to the marketplace then learning how to sell and do it well. So learn sales to succeed in business.

Masculinity Gives You Power With Women

There is no competition for masculine men. Women want to follow a strong masculine man and will follow him anywhere. The more masculine you are the more women will want you and the stronger that they will respond to you. This isn't a choice on their part but is biology at work. Remember attraction isn't a choice, it's a reaction. And nothing causes a stronger reaction in women than a masculine man. One who is dominant, takes charge, and never apologizes for himself. Just like a man but can't help to respond to long straight hair, a large bust, and built rear, it's not a choice.

You must embrace and cultivate your masculinity as well as have an understanding of women. Women are either going to be one of the greatest sources of fun and pleasure for you or the greatest source of misery and pain if you aren't masculine and don't understand them. Women can innately sense a man's power. His innate masculinity that is. Put simply the more masculine you are the more women are naturally going to do what you want and fall into your dominant strong frame. Be a masculine man and women will do whatever you want.

Combat Skills Give You Power In Life

At the end of the day the man who can't defend himself is a target. You could have all the money in the world as well as understand women completely yet a random thug could take everything from you if he wanted. You have to learn how to fight and defend yourself against predators. You have to know how to throw a punch, be aware to danger, as well as use a firearm. These aren't negotiable skills either, none of the skills in this chapter are. They are requirements to live a full life worth living. A life where you have freedom, as freedom stems from power.

If you're not proficient in these areas then you shouldn't rest until you are. That would be like being on the front line preparing for an enemy advance. Then resting even though the trench wasn't dug, the ammo wasn't stored, and your men weren't in position. It would only be a matter of time before you'd be overrun and killed. Never forget that there are others out there who if you are a target have no problem exploiting that. Just because we left the jungle doesn't mean our nature has changed. There will always be prey and predator.

Summary

So there you have it. Three ways to get power in three important areas of your life. The sooner you learn these skills and become proficient at them the better off you will be. Pursue power and there is a chance at freedom, pursue anything else and you'll never get freedom. This world is not your friend and you must conduct yourself accordingly. Don't be naive, be strong and you'll make it to where you want to go.

It's Your Duty To Become Powerful

If you give a shit about yourself, your immediate family, or your brothers then it is your duty to become powerful. Otherwise you'll have to stand by and watch as they are all torn apart and taken from you or if all you care for is yourself (which there is nothing wrong with) then you will torn apart and crushed by this earth. The world is not your friend. Without power you will be taken advantage of, without power you will be enslaved, without power you will be crushed. Without power you can do nothing. The world is cruel, dark, and harsh and will stab you mercilessly if you let your guard down even for a second.

Power is the only thing that will save you from a life of pain and suffering. Power, strength is the only thing you can put your trust in. Your own strength is the only thing that will never fail you. Your family will betray you, your wife stab you in the back, even your own children may turn against you. But your strength, your strength is the only thing that will never leave you. Your strength is the one thing you can count and rely on. Maybe a strong brother but no one else and even then who knows. Your own strength is the only thing you can put your faith in 100%.

Strength Is The Only Thing That Matters

With strength you can do anything, without strength you can do nothing. Strength is the only virtue, and weakness the only vice. Anyone who think otherwise is either living in denial or is living in a bubble. Both make for easy targets for the world. Strength, power, or whatever you want to call it, that is your only defense against the world. Your strength is to you what a lion's claws and teeth are to him. Without them he will be torn to shreds. Likewise without power so will you.

Never rely on the mercy of others like I said above even your family will stab you in the back if it's their own ass on the line. Survival is all there is. You own family would drown you in a lake if it interfered with their survival. Understand this. There are no friends when everyone gets hungry. Everyone around you will turn on you in a moment if things get hard. Be ready to strike them all down at a moment's notice. Never put your trust fully in someone, this doesn't mean paranoid. It means don't be a fool.

The Truth About People

You will not find mercy. Nor should you look for it.

Instead declare war on your weakness so that you will never be in need of mercy. You are either going to kill or get killed in this world. Be a killer. Strike before struck. Stop pretending that people around you wouldn't cut you to shreds in a second. People are weak and will do anything to not get swept away. Most of your "friends" would desert you if it meant social alienation or even a bit of discomfort. Hell even your parents would desert you if it meant a bit of discomfort not deserting you. People are weak and their weakness makes them untrustworthy.

If you have a few brothers who have their masculinity, honor, and pride in tact maybe just maybe they'll support you when things get tough but that's it. And even then you can never rely on others, ever. As I said above there is only one source of salvation, there is only one thing that will save you. And that is your own strength, your own power. Nothing more and nothing less. The strongest survive, always every time. No exceptions. Anyone who lives by any other is playing Russian roulette with fate. Who knows when they'll finally reach the bullet.

Strength The Only Virtue

This may sound harsh, good we live in a harsh world. Power the only thing that'll save you. Never rely on others, never trust others. Understand that everyone is operating from whatever is best for them. Your friends and family are no exceptions. Always be ready to cut the throat of the person next to you. Always be ready that they'll lunge at you to do the same any moment. Attaining power is your duty. Do it for yourself, do it so you won't get crushed, so you won't get eaten alive.

The earlier someone tells you this the better. And someone who is willing to shatter the delusion you live in to convey this information to you is a true friend. Be so powerful you can destroy anyone and everything around you and you won't get attacked. If you can cause someone to lose their career because of your influence in the community, could kick their ass because of your combat training, and could steal their wife/girlfriend if you wanted then you have nothing to fear from that person. Because you are more powerful then they are.

Summary

The only thing that truly matters in life is attaining more and more power. Everything else is secondary to that. With power you can afford to indulge in some delusions of the masses but when the gloves come off always be prepared for the reality of the world. Anyone who tells you anything but strength or power is what count is trying to weaken you to take advantage of you or is a fool. Either way they shouldn't be listened to. Become powerful, become strong. For strength is the only true virtue and weakness the only true vice.

What Is The Purpose Of Life For A Man?

What it the purpose of life? In particular what is the purpose of life for a man? Many throughout the ages have given different answers. Some would say strong sons that will carry on his name with pride, this is important but it is not all there is. Likewise others would say to acquire vast wealth, again good but not all. When you boil it down there is really one thing that defines a man, one thing that makes him stand out from the pack. And that one thing is strength.

Not necessarily strength of arm (though important) and certainly not how much he can bench press (don't make me laugh). But strength meaning power. The strength of the fire that burns in his heart. That fire that animates a man and makes him the highest of creation. The fire that every great man and warrior has felt. That fire that changes and shapes the world itself. That is the fire, the strength that I am talking about. Which brings us back to the question, what then is the purpose of a man's life?

Ascension

We were created to be more than we are. We were created to

constantly rise through conquering every challenge that life and our enemies would throw at us. We were created to take our pain and turn it into progress. To be thrown into the fire and come out steel. To constantly ascend to the next level. To constantly become more than we were the day before. To constantly fight against overwhelming odds. To stand against fate and even if everything is against us, fight boldly.

Life is about ascension. All the great stories tell of heroes who through pain, suffering, and fighting became something more than they ever thought they'd be. Many ascended to be demi-gods something between God and man. Something more. Being born with a Y chromosome makes you a male, ascending to be all that you can be makes you a man. As I've said in all my writings, manhood is something that is earned through sweat, trail, and blood. You can't become steel without going through the fire.

The Purpose Of A Man's Life

So here it is brothers the purpose of a man's life. The purpose of a man's life is to become the absolute strongest that he can be in all facets. To meet every day fighting and becoming better in some way, shape, or form. To look the great of evil and trouble in the eye and meet it with a smile. To most this would sound corny or cheesy because they live in sheltered little bubbles. But for true men this will resonate with something deep down in your spirit. Something primal, something noble, and something fierce.

The purpose of life is to become the strongest that we can be. Strength is what matters in the end. Everything else burns away but strength. With strength you can defy the universe without strength you will always be a pawn to be used and discarded like a worn out whore. The universe and others will have no pity for you. But you should despise pity anyways. You should want to face the greatest challenges that there is, because in overcoming great challenges we become great men.

Look To The Heavens

A man's focus should be on pursing the unattainable goal. The become like his creator. This is the greatest honor one can give. Man has been given the choice to ascend towards the angels or descend towards the beasts (and honestly modern man has sunk below the level of the beast). This is the greatest gift we were given. Even the gods themselves envied mortals for this. We have been given a choice, greatness or nothing. It all depends on how we conduct ourselves. The more we overcome the stronger we become.

Seek challenge, seek "pain". Not pain as in self-inflicted pain but the good kind of pain. The kind of pain that comes from straining, fighting, and growing. Meet every day to conquer it. Strive to overcome a greater and greater challenge every day. Life is about constant ascension, constant fighting, and constant growth. When all is said and done it will be this that matters. Become the most powerful you can be, that is the purpose of life.

Summary

Seek challenge. Seek it every day until what once challenged you is child's play…and then seek an even greater challenge. Comfort is a lie that will destroy you. The strongest survive, if there's one truth that holds true in this world that is it. Force yourself through the strongest fire so you can become what others will only dream about. Do what others would never do so you become what others will never become. That is the purpose of life. Become better every day.

How To Have Masculine Body Language

In a previous chapter we talked about how to talk like a man now it's time to learn how to walk (or stand…or sit) like a man. Both a woman's attraction for you as well as how much respect a man is going to have from you comes from your body language. Believe it or not but most of communication is communicated through body language. What we actually say only makes up about seven percent or so. Our body language speaks louder than our words ever could. If a guy has bad (feminine) body language it's going to be a turn off for women and he's going to have trouble getting respect from other men.

In this chapter I'm going to lay out the basics of masculine body language. Follow this guide is going to help you look more masculine and help convey your masculinity to others. Don't be surprised if after following this for some time you start getting stares from chicks, a masculine man stands out like nothing else. You'll also feel more masculine once adopting this body language. It works together to form a positive cycle. The more masculine you feel the easier it is to adopt masculine body language and vice versa. A good cycle to be in. Alright now for how to have masculine body language.

It's A Process

First off reading this chapter one time isn't going to be enough to undo years of bad conditioning. Just like redoing old negative thought patterns, it's going to take some time. You can't just change your stance once and expect for it to stick forever more. However the more you correct yourself the more that the pattern of masculine body language is going to get lodged into your brain. So it takes time but at the same time the more you do it the less you have to worry about it. Think of it like you would any other habit.

It takes time but once in place you don't have to worry about it anymore. So what you're going to want to do at first is at certain take note of what you're doing with your body. So for example before going out for a night look in the mirror and practice holding good body language for a couple of minutes. That way your mind is going to get a feeling for how it feels and it'll make it easier to snap into it when you're out and about. Again remember this will eventually become a habit once you get over that learning curve.

Take Up Space

Alright first things first, take up space. Stand with your feet at least should length apart. Uncross your arms and don't cross your legs. Drape your arm over the seat next to you and so on and so forth. When you're out you want to think expansion. Take up as much space as possible. Not to the point that you look like a clown of course but you want to expand into the environment instead of retract from it. This is just like a man takes action and effects the world around him instead of being affected by it but in physical form.

I'll give you two examples for reference. One is you standing at the bar. You should have your drink out away from you not right up next to your chest like your hiding. You don't want there to be anything between your vulnerable parts (neck, groin, chest) and the world. This shows confidence and masculinity on a primal level. Your head should be up and your movements should be slowed and controlled, no jerky nervous movements. Another example is when seated. Your arm should be resting on the chair next to you or back of the couch, open up. Likewise your legs should planted firmly apart and not crossed. Open, expansion, exposing.

Walk With Pride

If you had a good father he no doubt told you at times to keep your chin up and your back straight. This is because he cared about how you presented yourself to the world and wanted you to present yourself with pride. Walk with your head high, shoulders back, and back straight. Don't slouch. Keep your chin a little in the air. Never look down as others pass, this signals submissiveness (which is the opposite of masculine). You want to also make sure that when you meet someone that you are looking them in the eyes directly and not looking down or too the side.

You want your chest to be high meaning your shoulders are pulled back. A good way of putting it is imagine your chest is light beams like on a car and you're trying to shine them in people's faces. Not slouching is something that plagues males more and more as their level of physical fitness goes down as well as they spend more and more time slouched over staring at a screen. Both for work and recreation. Remember chest up, chin up, back straight, and shoulders back. Write yourself a reminder to put on your mirror if you have to.

Summary

Alright so there you have it the basics of masculine body language. It'll take time to get down but once you get it down you'll be amazed at who notices. When you have masculine body language you stand out and in a good way. Without even speaking a word you convey that you are a man among boys. You convey your strength and dominance to the world in a natural way that everyone innately responds to on a primal level. Remember most of our communication is through body language.

No One Can Go Through The Fire For You

In business I'm all about outsourcing. Do whatever is the best use of your time. Why mow your lawn when you're making over one hundred dollars and hour? Why go get coffee? Why wash your car. Time is your most valuable asset and you would be wise to always make the most out of it. Don't be that guy who makes six figures but will sit there and argue with a company on the phone for forty five minutes to save twenty bucks. You can't nickel

and dime your way to
riches anyways.

However with that being said
there are many things in life that you
have to do yourself. There are things
that others cannot do for you and
that you must take responsibility for.
Especially when it comes to
masculinity and being a man. A
good part of being a man is taking
responsibility for yourself and your
life. To take the lead and to take
action to get the things that you want
in life. There are paths that you must
take that can only be walked alone.

Initiation Into Manhood

A great example of this is most
tribal society's rites of initiation.

This not something that can be outsourced, it is not something that a boy's father, mother, brother, or other tribe member can do for him. He must do it himself. But he does this so he can attain his manhood. He sees what lies on the other side that makes it all worth it. Even if he is scared, even if he's in pain, he still walks the path alone because he knows it's part of becoming a man.

The same can be said of you and me. There will be times in our life when no one not even our closest friends or family will be able to help us. There will be battles that we must face on our own with no help. There comes times when it's just us against the world. And it is these times that will truly try and test us. However without these times of fire we could never become the strongest of steel the is masculinity. Good does not come from easy.

Testing Of Our Mettle

It's good to have a network of good men that have your back, a tribe so to speak. However that doesn't mean you can afford to get soft or allow your tribe members to pick up your slack. You must always be striving to become the best that you can possibly be. Constant ascension as I often talk about. All men on this earth bear scars from fights that they had to face alone.

Others may have had their back or supported them but it was them who had to enter the cave and fight their way out the other side. It was them who had to face it alone.

However when we come out the other side we are forever changed. There is no shortcut to this fundamental change, it is something we all discover on our own in our own time. Some discover it the hard way others are warned by other so they take matters into their own hands. Some go through this change by one close to them dying, others through the breaking of a marriage, others through losing a child. Everyone comes to that cave from a different direction. But everyone has to pass through it alone.

Independence Before Interdependence

For interdependence to work everyone who is part of it must be independent themselves. And independence is derived from strength. You have to go through the abyss before you can come out the other side stronger. There are demons that we have to face and slay alone. We can talk about the fight and the demon to other men but the actual fight is going to be one on one. Because of this, because you will have to face challenges on your own. You have to make sure that you can stand on your own two feet and meet whatever the world is going to throw at you.

To attain the rank of man you have to be tested by the fire. Man is not something you biologically become like the way a girl biologically matures into a woman. Like I've said in my books manhood is earned and many males will go to their graves having never earned it. It cannot be earned by another and given to you. You must go out and earn it yourself. You must slay your demon yourself. All on your own. Stop relying on others for the most important things in life.

Summary

A man must always be prepared to face the next challenge on his own. He must cultivate his strength so that even without anyone else he will still rise and conquer. If you want to be the king then you must go through everything that is required to be a king. There is no outsourcing for masculinity or leadership. Go through the fire you will be better for it and you will have earned your place among the ranks of men.

How To Be A High Value Man

Our duty in this life is to become the very best that we can be in every facet of our lives. To become stronger and better every day. To go from battle to battle even war to war greater than we were before. We are to take both victory and defeat in stride not letting either deter us from our ultimate goal of ascension. When I speak in this chapter of being a high value man I'm not talking about being attractive to women (though a high value man will be incredibly attractive to women) that is a goal that a man shouldn't focus on. That will come as a byproduct of pursuing your ultimate goals.

When I say a high value man I mean a man that is high value to his brothers, his flag, and yes women as well. But above all he is high value to himself. He has high value to the tribe, he has high survival value. He can take whatever challenge comes his way. His value to the tribe is unmistakable. He excels in every aspect. His strength, courage, cunning, ferocity, and wisdom are all unmatched. He is a man among men, he is a high value man. He is a man striving to echo the best that there is. A man who wants to become more than he is day in and day out. Now how to become a high value man.

Grow The Mind

We shall start with the mind. A man must take hold of his mind and use it to serve him. He must master his mind as well as grow it. His mind was made for expansion on all fronts. A mind that does not grow dies. The high value man seeks out wisdom and knowledge. He looks at those who have come before and learns from them while always listening to his guy and inner wisdom. He knows that his mind is one of his greatest gifts and that to honor this he must make the most out of it.

He is always reading and gaining knowledge. Because he knows knowledge is power and that it is his duty to become powerful because nothing in this world (for good or ill) is gained without power and strength. He also builds his willpower. He knows that the body follows the mind. When things get tough he has learned to keep grinding and push past discomfort. His body has become the servant of his mind as it should be. He can push past exhaustion and fear to accomplish that tasks that are set before him. While others run he grits down and marches forward. He has disciplined himself.

Harden The Body

With this being said the high value man still understands that while the body may be servant to the mind it is still important. He does not neglect his body. He understands that his body is a tool to accomplish his will in this world and like any strong man keeps his tool in good working order. A good soldier knows to keep his weapon clean and in working order at all times. Likewise does the high value man do the same with his body. He doesn't become obsessed with his body as weak man are prone to do.

Rather he recognizes it for the tool that it is.

He conditions it and makes sure that goodness goes into it. Just like he feeds his mind with good information he feeds his body with good food and drink. He exercises, trains, dresses properly, and maintains his strength. He trains his body so that it acts on command. So that his reflexes are automatic. He drills until he can't drill anymore. He etches the drills he needs to survive and fight. For a hard body that cannot be put to use is as worthless as a weak body. The high value man knows how to apply his body against others to defend himself and others, to get what he wants.

Lift The Spirit

Now we go to the deepest level. Something that truly separates the high value man from all other men. He has a connection with something much deeper and stronger than himself. His connection to The Pater God, his inner masculinity, his inner fire he cultivates and holds dear. He pride and strength are born here. He fight is as well. He knows that the worst thing that can happen is that this fire that burns within him be extinguished. Better he be dead then to lose this fire. It is this fire that makes him a man. This animating spirit from the divine.

To cultivate this spirit he constantly seeks to be stronger as strength is one of the greatest representations of that fire that there is. He has fellowship with other men, with brothers. He'd rather be alone than in the company of the weak and degenerate. He learns of heroes and great men that expressed this fire with every breath that they took. He seeks to live the same live and have such an impact on the world. When he looks in the mirror he can see this fire in his eyes, his can feel it in his bones. It's hard to describe but unmistakable when felt.

This spirit is grown through suffering, developing strength, and closeness to the All-Father.

Summary

In a world of high value men there is no evil. There are wars sure but not evil. The only way things will get better is if more males become high value men. These are the leaders of men. The great heroes and kings that we used to honor and that all the old tales are about. The purpose of life is constant struggle, constant ascension. We all must strive to be high value men. To be strong, powerful, wise, and mighty to be the closest echo we can of our creator, that is the greatest honor.

Grow the fire greater day by day and you will become a high value man, this is assured.

The Only Two Things A Man Can Trust

Trust me! No trust me! Well of course you can trust me! We are bombarded with different groups and people telling us that it's fine to trust them. That they "have our backs" and (hard to say this without laughing) "have our best interests at heart". From politicians, to corporations with advertisements, to women, to pretty much anything and everyone else we are told that we should trust. Our parents tell us to trust them to believe that they know what they are talking about and know what they are doing.

Our preachers and teachers ask the same thing of us. As does of school system as does our boss. Trust that I'm not a complete piece of shit who won't work you like a dog until you collapse and then you to the wayside for the next eager slave. Trust in our world is given out like candy, and then men wonder while charlatans are so rampant. Why a clown who can talk well will go one hundred times farther than an honorable strong man who doesn't know how to talk so well. A dog species that exposed it's neck to every new dog it met would so go extinct because of how many dogs would rip it's throat out. The same can be said of males who give their trust in things not worthy of it. Here are two things a man can trust.

First & Foremost – His Own Strength

Your own strength is the only thing on this earth that you can put complete one hundred percent trust in. You strength will never leave you nor forsake you. Your strength is always with you and can always be used to get out of where you are. That's why the most important thing you can do in this world is develop you strength. Your friends, family, society, women, religion, government, and everything else will leave you and cannot be relied upon but your strength can. Your strength is the only thing in this world you can put your unfailing faith in, the only thing.

You must develop this strength on all fronts. Strength of arm, strength of mind, strength of spirit. You must master the skills needed to survive in any environment. The world will try and test you and do it's best to beat you down and have you go back to the slave pens with your tail tucked between your legs. It is only through your strength that this can be prevented, it is only through your strength that you will make it. And when I say strength I don't mean how much you can bench press (though physical strength is one component of strength) rather I mean your entire strength as a man. The strongest of which will be something deep within you.

Second – Vetted Honorable Brothers

These are members of your tribe and brotherhood that have been vetted. Meaning that they've been tried by the fire and proven themselves to you time and time again. They have strength and honor and your respect. This isn't given out freely. Just because someone is part of your group does not mean that they are worthy of your trust. Trust like respect must be earned. And even then they must prove themselves day in and day out. Men get sidetracked and waylaid. Even men that we thought were strong can have an Achilles heel that could be their undoing as well as your own if you place your trust in them.

However there are those few brothers who we know would have our back and place honor above all else. They are few and far in between but they are there. I should note that Westerner's make a mockery of this as well. How many kids have you heard say to another

"You're my brother" or "You're family" maybe they've watched too many movies or something but they fail to understand what those words truly mean. I've had kids call me "brother" before and I told them to fuck off and that I wasn't their "brother". But I also have a few choice friends where this description is proper and who I do trust and trust deeply.

What Not To Put Your Trust In

I want to make it clear just because you don't place your trust fully in something doesn't mean you hate it. For example to fully trust your child to be able to have your back would be foolish as they are a child and incapable of doing so. Does this mean that you hate your child? Of course not, you love your child. But you love your child for who they are, taking into account their limitations. So just because I say something isn't worthy of your trust does not therefore mean it's worthy of your scorn or hatred (though some are).

Weak males cannot be trusted. Of all things weak males are the most untrustworthy, they are even worse than women. Weak males will stab you in the back, lie, cheat, and steal to get ahead of you. Never trust a weak male, they are the most pathetic of creatures. Women, this one is obvious. A woman will do whatever her emotions tell her to do in the moment. Contracts and masculine ideals such as honor have no place in a woman's mind and mean nothing to her. She'll do what feels good when it feels good every time is she can get away with it. Not something worthy of your trust.

Governments, religions, and family. The first two are specifically made to make you a slave and weak. The latter has been programmed by the first two to get you to love your slavery. Corporations and the education system. Corporations do not have profits as their first concern despite what uninformed hippies will tell you. If they did they wouldn't push so hard for political ideals that alienate their customers. Corporations are a tool of those in power to push agendas that are bad for you and good for them. The exact same thing can be said of the education system.

Summary

In the end as important as it is to have a strong group of men (something that is becoming more and more rare as time goes on) you ultimately you are on your own and can only rely on your strength. Which is why I push so hard for men to develop their strength. You cannot rely on others even your brothers will get sick of carrying your weight and you certainly can't rely on the corporation you work for, the government you pay taxes too, or the religion you worship to help you out. You must cultivate enough strength so that you can be self-reliant. Self-reliance is not an option but rather a necessity for a man.

I almost forgot. Technically there are three things a man can trust. His own strength, vetted honorable brothers, and his dog.

Stoicism & Masculinity

Stoicism and masculinity go together like two peas in a pod. They are inseparable from one another. Like being nurturing and femininity. Masculine men are very stoic and vice versa. Nowadays males have been taught to be affected by the world around them in the way that a woman would (it makes them easier to control). Males have been taught it's okay to be a victim, it's okay to let their emotions control them, and that "keeping a stiff upper lip" is an "outdated term" (out dated apparently being a term for "making it harder to push our agenda).

The fact of the matter is none of this is true. Men were meant to be stoic and strong. While this makes them harder to control and mislead (bad news for those at the top) it makes them men and much more successful in their own lives. Men were made to be unaffected by the world around them, the be stronger than the circumstances thrust upon them, to overcome, to advance, to conquer. To be hit hard and barely even register it. That is to be a man.

What Stoicism Is Not

Now with this being said I want to make sure you don't get the wrong idea so I'm going to discuss what stoicism is not. Stoicism is not being a doormat. It's not letting others walk all over you while you remain unaffected. It's not allowing a woman to beat and berate you without reacting. It's not being emotionless and it's not retreating from the world into a shell. Many would have you believe that is what stoicism is so that you miss out on the great power that stoicism give you.

Stoicism is strength. It's not bending to the will of others and being so strong you push right through adversity. Stoicism is not giving in to your emotions and weaker desires but keeping on. It's not flinching when you take a hit (though you do retaliate). It's not turning the other cheek but rather being a strong unassailable wall. That no matter what the enemy throws at you it has no effect because of the strength of the wall. Stoicism means you affect the world around you more than you are affected by it. That you stand strong in the face of adversity and do not back down, cower, or run away.

The Oak

A good metaphor for stoicism is the oak and the storm. The oak is one of the mightiest of trees. The roots are deep and the tree is strong.

When the storm comes and the rain beats down the oak is unaffected. When the winds blow harder and harder the oak is unaffected. No matter what the storm throws at the oak it will not be uprooted it will weather the toughest of storms and come out stronger. Adversity does not faze it. It laughs at the attempts to uproot and destroy it. For it knows its roots are deep and its base strong.

Men are to be their own oak. They are to weather the storms of life unaffected by them. They are as Kipling so eloquently put keeping their heads about them while everyone around them is losing theirs. When the guns start firing and the bombs dropping you remain unaffected but rather do what must be done. What goes on outside doesn't matter because you have what is going inside under control and you know with that you can meet any challenge. The stoic take action, they are not passive, they are unaffected by adversity not unresponsive to it.

The Wall Upon Which The World Breaks

A man is the wall upon which the world breaks. A man doesn't get emotional when things happen rather he rushes forward and takes the actions that must be taken. He does what must be done unaffected by the chaos around him. No matter the blow he takes he keeps moving forward. No matter what this world throws at him the stoic man keeps forward ascending to greater and greater heights with every step. He does not let anything deter him from his ultimate goal.

Stoicism is also not that foolish philosophy that says nothing is either good nor bad and to just sit back and wait. A man is active not passive. Sitting back and rationalizing everything is for fools. A man is the mountain unaffected and unconquered by all around it. He rises strong for all to see. The world around the mountain may pass away and be destroyed completely but the mountain will remain strong and unaffected. Let the winds blow, lightning strike, and the storm do what it will. The mountain will always and forever remain the mountain.

Summary

Oak, mountain, rock these have all been used to describe men and for good reason. These things aren't affected by the environment around it. They are the opposite of weak substances that conform to whatever they are put in. A good analogy to being a man. The world conforms to a man not the other way around. A man through his strength of arm, mind, and heart forges the world around him to what he wants it to be. He is an active part of the world. He makes his mark upon the world while the world cannot leave a scratch on him. Affect the world while remaining unaffected by it.

How To Form An Honor Group

Men need an honor group. A brotherhood, an alliance, a tribe, a gang, a "family", a wolf pack. Call it what you will but it's essential for men to develop relations with other men, other strong honorable men. This isn't say that a man cannot be strong on his own or that he should use others as an excuse to not develop himself. Take responsibility for yourself and for where you are at in life at all times. An honor group serves as a way to make you even stronger through testing and challenge.

Men who have honor groups come out much stronger and sharper than the average male who is cut off from other males. A male who has only his wife is going to have a very hard time becoming better and strong on his own. He needs other to push him and make him better. As the wise man once said "As iron sharpens iron, so does one man sharpen another". Finding brothers in a world of effeminate weaklings is not easy but it can be done. Here I am going to show you how to forge your own honor group.

Standards

First things first there needs to be standards. Accepting everybody automatically means that your group will not be honorable. These standards don't have to be based on religion, race, or physical characteristics (though they may be). It could be on simply swearing an oath to develop oneself to the utmost of their abilities. It could be through achieving certain combat adeptness. It's up to you to make the standards but there must be standards. It could be anything from you both share similar interests and beliefs to having a certain bloodline. I'll leave this up to you.

The point is no anyone and everyone can join. And once it is formed new members must be vetted by current members. This doesn't mean that one lone asshole can screw up the entire process but rather that some sort of agreement is reached. One can't just show up with two pieces of shit and say "Hey they're part of the group now". Your place in the group must be earned.

So here are two prerequisites for forming an honor group. First off not everyone can be allowed to join. There must be some sort of discriminating process in place. Like I said it could be based on strength, heart, or any number of factors but not everyone can be allowed to join. Second for new members to enter there must be some sort of agreement from the old members and then there must be a trial period. No one can just waltz on in or with the approval of one member. No special favors.

No Women

For honor to exist in a group women cannot have a say. Once women have a say in the group the dynamic changes and honor goes out the window. An honor group must be male only. It is only the male of the human species that has honor. This isn't to insult women simply to state a fact. It's not that women are evil but they are not honorable. It is a masculine concept only understood by strong masculine men. Have your women but they are not to be involved in the honor group. This isn't a suggestion, this is a must.

Like I said once women are introduced into the group everything changes. Even them being present will change things. Honor groups are for men and men alone. The meetings, bonding, and brotherhood takes place between men without the presence of women. Honor groups are male only spaces. This is non-negotiable. And if anyone in the group suggests to allow women in you are best off expelling him from the group in order to maintain the integrity of the groups honor.

Honor & Shame

Being an honor group obviously honor is going to play a large part. Honor being the standards that you hold the group accountable too (this is different from the standards that are required to enter into the group). For example you could require reading, combat training, and weekly meetings as part of staying in the group. And those who didn't comply would be shamed. A guy who entered into the group out of shape would be shamed until he was in shape. Likewise the weak male who entered the group would be shamed until he became strong.

Shame is powerful when wielded by honorable men with the

intent to improve the men around them. This same shame is destructive when wielded by women or the state who use it to make men their slaves. But that's a topic for another time. If ninety nine percent of people offered me advice I'd probably tell them to "fuck off" but when a member of my honor group tells me something I listen. I listen because I respect them and understand where it's coming from. Don't get me wrong at the end of the day I'm still my own man but I respect the word of my honor group.

Summary

Now the challenge is finding males who are worthy of entrance into your group. And for this I suggest you search far and wide. You are more likely to find strong honorable men in certain places then others. Look for places that cater more to men. Maybe an old dive bar, the gym, or a cigar bar. These are just suggestions. You'll have to adjust depending on where you live. Regardless find men that will test and better you. That will hold you accountable and not give you any slack. Find an honor group.

The Original Sin

All of mankind's problems can be traced back to a single fateful event. All the pain, suffering, plagues, death, and destruction coming from one event. We see this same thing happening today. Pain, suffering, and destructing coming from this source. So what is this source? This destroyer of civilizations and mighty kingdoms? The thing that started it all in the first place? There are a few certain words that we could use and depending on the reason even more. But the original sin can be traced back to one thing, one man's weakness.

One man's weakness allowed evil to enter into the world, just like today the weakness of "men" allows feminism to run rampant, our elites to scorn us openly, and an unopposed invasion to sweep throughout the land. Modern males have placed being accepted and "nice" above being honorable and strong. They have embraced weakness and the world will crumble because of it. These males not realizing that everything that is being thrown at them (from feminism to mockery to invasion) are essential giant shit tests.

These males have responded in the one way you never respond

when someone tries you. They groveled even harder thinking their salvation came from licking boot that much harder. Modern males are a prime example of this they worship women and grovel before the enemy expecting that it will inspire kindness from them. Weakness in men is pathetic and only inspires hatred and disgust as it rightly should. It's as if the modern male wishes to be a female where groveling inspires mercy and that they wish for females to be males to make up for their own lack of masculinity.

The Original Sin

As the story goes once man lived in paradise. He walked with the creator and lived in a perfect setting. Then woman was introduced. And they lived peacefully for some time. But then women (or in this case woman) being women were led into temptation by the deceiver. Then she went to her husband and threw a test at him to see if he was weak and pathetic enough to do the same. Now man was faced with a choice hold on to his balls and his honor and do justice to the woman and honor his creator or be a weak little bitch and follow his wife's lead.

He chose to be a weak little bitch and mankind has suffered ever since. All because one "man" choose to follow his wife over his honor. Choose to follow women over God. He showed weakness and was rightly crucified for it. Any man who follows a woman deserves the same fate. Following and submitting to woman is the greatest of sins and one only the most pathetic of males commit. A man submitting to and listening to a female is an unnatural, abhorrent, despicable, loathsome, horrible, and a whole thesaurus worth of words act.

Man Leads, Women Submits

A male who submits to a woman will never be a man. Plain and simply. He could have conquered hundreds of countries be worth billions and have a mind that rivaled the smartest males who have ever lived yet he would still be a boy and not worthy of respect. Putting women/a woman above one's own pride, honor, and dignity is the lowest level a man can sink to. Trying to appease women is the same as submitting to them. It's disgusting and abhorrent. The modern male lacks any pride or balls, so he submits, grovels, and tries to appease instead of standing firm and putting others in their place.

Appeasement is a sin. As is listening to or submitting to a woman. Foolish is the man who listens to a woman and it is obvious he doesn't understand them. Only the weakest of males would let themselves be led around by a woman and women know this. Strength is what women respond to, strength is what the world responds to. Any male who gives a woman's word as much weight as his own is a fool. And will be destroyed like all fools eventually are. Adam should have honored both himself and his creator and taken care of both Eve and the deceiver like a man and none of us would be in this mess in the first place.

Summary

Submitting to, appeasing, or listening to women or your enemy are all sins of the highest order. A man leads and follows his own wisdom. He puts both women and his enemies in their place. He doesn't fall for their tricks or lies. And he certainly doesn't try to do things their way or grovel before them. Weakness is evil and despicable. Especially in males. All evil comes from the weakness of males. Never put a woman before your own self, honor, pride, creator, or brothers. Likewise appeasement always ends up in you getting it twice as hard. Don't appease fight and stand like a man.

Take Pride In Yourself

A man takes pride in himself and who he is. The destroyers of civilization would have you believe that pride is an evil, that pride is some sort of vice. They tell you this because they hate honor and know that a man who takes pride in himself will stand up for himself and what he believes in. Free men have pride while slaves do not. They tell you pride is evil to make a slave out of you, to make your docile, complacent, put simply to make you an easy mark an easy target so they can do what they want with you.

It'd be like a wolf telling all the deer that not having a broken leg was evil and wrong. Only the dumbest believe what their enemy tells them, unfortunately most men have no idea who the enemy is or that there even is one. They fail to see that the society around them is a bigger threat to them than any far off army or bugaboo that the destroyers of civilization push. A man who takes pride in himself and who he is expands his strength and thereby his honor. He becomes an example to lead the other slaves out of captivity, something that the rulers do not want.

Take Pride In Yourself

A man takes pride in himself. He takes pride in who he is, what he stands for, and what he is about. Pride is good, pride is noble, and pride is honorable. By pride I don't mean arrogance but rather pride as in being proud of oneself. A man who has pride in himself does not bow to others or go along with whatever they want. He stands his ground and is firm in his beliefs. He cannot be pushed around by the world or controlled. He is self-reliant, he is independent, he is free. And it is this kind of man that can undo the entire matrix. Which is society does everything in its power to thwart this kind of man from ever developing.

Take pride in yourself, take pride in who you are, take pride in your race, take pride in your heritage, take pride in being a man, take pride in standing strong and fighting against the world around you. While others wallow about in weakness and degeneracy like pigs in mud you stand above. While others stuff their face you train, while others whack off to porn you attract the most beautiful and desirable women, while others are decaying you are growing stronger every day. Take pride in this, take pride in yourself, and take pride in being a man.

High Standard

A man holds himself to a high standard. I hold myself to a standard this is unreachable. I do this because I want to be sure that no one else will hold me to a higher standard then I hold myself. I do this because I have pride in myself and want to be the best. I want to put myself through the deepest of fires so that when the world throws its own fires at me they'll barely even register. It'd be like if you had to fight a man your size and practiced on yourself and held yourself to a standard where you fought and beat men who stood a foot taller then you and weight one hundred pounds more. When the fight came it'd be a joke.

Hold yourself to such a standard that even the hardest and strongest of men couldn't hold you to a higher one. Go above and beyond whatever you think is necessary day in and day out. That is how you become strong, that is how you become a man, that is how you become the best. Let's say that society expects you to operate at a level of 5 (using numbers to explain the concept better), your honor group expects you to operate at a level of 25, and your father expects you to operate at a level of 30, and your greatest hero operated at a level of 75. Hold yourself to the standard of someone who operates at a level of 100.

Do Hard Things

If something is hard then it's probably the right thing to do. If you have a choice between two decision and are wondering which one is the right one. It's a good bet whichever one is harder to do is going to be the right choice. The one that causes more discomfort, pain, and thereby growth. Choose the harder right over the easier wrong. Force yourself to do things you don't want to do. Discipline works like a muscle, the more you use it the stronger it will get. Force yourself to wake up early instead of sleeping in, to hit the gym instead of watch TV, to read a book instead of using social media. And so on and so forth.

By constantly doing hard things you will constantly better yourself. You will become better than those around you and ascend to higher and higher levels. Move against resistance, move against inertia, that is how you become stronger. Fight against the current. Seek out others who are like minded and will add to your progress. You will be fought against and others will try to push you back into mediocrity. They do this because either your growth will show them how weak they are or they fear you growing because you'll break the chains they have binded you with. Taking flak is a good indication that you are on target.

Summary

Take pride in yourself and who you are. Take pride in your heritage and in being a man. Hold yourself to a high standard, higher than anyone else around you can or would hold you to. Do hard things, fight against inertia and weakness. That is how you become strong. Understand that most will wish that you always remain a slave, a eunuch, a castrated spineless wimp. But that is not how a man was born to live. A man was born to live proud and free. Never forget this.

Remember Who You Are

One of my favorite movies of all time is *The Lion King*. I watched it many times as a boy. *The Lion King* is a great move and should be watched by every boy. In particular there is one scene that always stood out to me (well two but we'll get to that later). It's where Simba meets with the monkey and the monkey leads him to his father. Simba has forgotten who he was and needed to be reminded by his father who he is. The one and true king.

I feel males in today's day and age are in a similar boat. They have forgotten who they are. They have been told lies from all sides designed to strip them of the thing that makes them a man, their power. A man without his power might as well not even be a man. A lion can be picked on by a mouse if the lions mind is neutered. A man with his masculinity intact is the most powerful force on this earth and anyone who tells you otherwise is full of shit.

Remember Who You Are

We have forgotten who we are. We have forgotten that we share the same lineage and capacity as the great warriors and kings of old. What one man can do another can do. Now we are taught day and night that we are nothing but victims and that we might as well not even try. We are told this because us (meaning men) are the only ones who have power to change anything. Men together can overturn any system and conquer any enemy. But first they must possess their masculinity and masculine power.

You are not powerless despite what society and bitter males tell you. As a matter of fact you are more powerful than you can imagine. You are capable of so much more than you can imagine. Man is the pinnacle of creation. Do you get that? The pinnacle meaning the top. Yet males act as if they are lowly worms or incapable of changing anything. These are lies, lies designed to keep you in chains. The road to developing your masculinity is a long and arduous one but it is worth every step. Remember who you are, you are powerful if you choose to develop that innate power within you.

Power & Majesty

If I could choose two words to describe masculinity I would use power and majesty. Power and majesty represent so much of what masculinity is. These are two words that are also used to describe God as in the Pater or Father God. This is no coincidence. Man was created to reflect the highest of all. He was created to be a mirror to the power of that highest power in existence. The be both powerful and majestic. Like a lion. This is your true calling. Is your time really well spent debating with feminists about how masculinity isn't evil? Do you think God debates with those who doubt him?

Of course not for they are so far below him that their doubt or lies mean nothing. It should be the same with you and feminists or other assorted cancers of our society. Arguing against them gives them validation, instead you should be developing yourself. Once you are developed others will naturally follow you. People are attracted to masculine power like bees to honey. Other males want to follow it and women want to be possessed by it. It's an energy in the air. It's something that resonates from deep within you. From the very core of your being. Men have forgotten what this is like and have forgotten who they are. Like a king in exile. Like Mufasa says in the scene referenced above we have forgotten who we are, we are more than what we have become, we are the true kings of this earth. It is time men reclaimed their place in the circle of life and got off the sidelines.

What Is The Wolf To The Lion

We live in a time of wolves I have no doubt about that. But I would further add what is a wolf to the lion? What are the forces of this world compared to the power of man? Nothing. You may not believe this and I can't say I blame you. Being stripped of your power it is hard to think about having full strength especially when most have never possessed it in the first place. But great things can come from humble beginnings. The richest men have come from the poorest slums, the greatest warriors from the weakest younglings, the greatest minds from those thought dumb.

Men must remember who they are. Remember that is they who have the power. Male power is no myth but rather reality. It's about time we reclaimed and used it to our own ends. You are not a victim unless you make yourself one. If the lion sits there and lets the hyenas take his kingdom and do as they please who can blame them? It's the lions own fault for not rising up and tearing them apart. The forces that are against men can be conquered. Every issue in your own life can be conquered for the men who take possession of this power and remember who they are. Who remember what they were created to be.

Summary

At the intro of this chapter I talked about another scene that stood out to me and it is where Simba has reclaimed his kingdom from his evil uncle and ascends to his rightful place as ruler of all around him. Like a man's rightful place is ruler of all around him. Men must embrace their dominance and reclaim the throne. They must be kings of their worlds. They must cast off this negativity and victim mindset and replace it with the journey to reclaim their masculine power.

You can either reclaim your throne or watch your kingdom be taken apart in front of you. I've said it before but it bears repeating as a man you don't have the option to just survive. You either thrive and become the king or you are cast out as a slave. Men operate at the highest level and lowest level. The comfortable middle is not part of manhood. Men either rise to the top or sink to the bottom. Sink or swim. It is your choice.

About The Author

Enjoyed the content? Then could you do me a favor? Leave a review on Amazon or tell a friend about the ways that the book has helped you. I love reading how my books have positively affected the lives of my readers. I read each and every review, they mean a lot to me. If you want to learn more I run a blog at charlessledge.com where you can find more content to further your masculine development to new heights. If you found value in the book drop by and join the community. Looking forward to hearing from you.

-Charles Sledge